WILD EDIBLE PLANTS OF TEXAS

LOCATE, IDENTIFY, STORE AND PREPARE YOUR FORAGED FINDS

FORAGED FINDS IN THE USA

SHANNON WARNER

Shannon Warner is a long-time forager and survivalist with a deep love for the outdoors. She has spent countless hours exploring the wilderness, learning about the plants and animals that inhabit it, and honing her skills in sustainable harvesting and ethical foraging. She has embarked on many adventures with her two loyal dogs by her side, from hiking and camping to hunting and fishing.

One of her core beliefs is in sustainable harvesting and ethical foraging. She firmly believes that it is possible to enjoy the bounty of nature without causing harm to the environment or depleting its resources. In her books, she provides practical tips and advice on how to forage in a way that is both sustainable and respectful of the natural world.

Whether you are an experienced forager or a beginner looking to learn more about the plants that grow in your backyard, Shannon's books are an invaluable resource that will inspire and inform you. With her expert guidance, you, too, can discover the many benefits of wild edible plants and unlock the secrets of the natural world.

ALSO BY SHANNON WARNER

<u>**Individual Regions**</u>

Wild Edible Plants of the Mid-Atlantic

Wild Edible Plants of California

Wild Edible Plants of the Pacific Northwest

Wild Edible Plants of the Southwest

<u>**2-Book Bundles**</u>

Wild Edibles of the West Coast

Foraging the Wild South

To Sonia,

Thank you for always listening to me and letting me run ideas by you, even when you have no idea what I'm talking about!

INTRODUCTION

Welcome to your one-stop guide to the fantastic world of foraging in the great state of Texas! You're about to start an exciting journey filled with adventure, delicious flavors, and a whole lot of fun. Texas is known for its incredible landscapes and unique cultures, and now you'll get to explore the wild side of this beautiful state through its wild edibles. So, buckle up and get ready for an unforgettable ride!

Texas is massive, and with its size comes various landscapes. From the lush forests of East Texas to the rolling hills of Central Texas, the warm Gulf Coast to the breathtaking deserts of West Texas, there's a whole lot to discover. Each region has unique flavors and foraging hotspots, making Texas a treasure trove for folks who love exploring and tasting the great outdoors. And the best part? You don't need to be an expert to join in on the fun!

One of the most incredible things about foraging is that it's an activity that anyone can enjoy. You might be a total beginner or someone with a bit of experience, but either way, there's always something new to learn and taste. And don't worry – this book will be your trusty guide through it all. We'll cover everything you need to know, from identifying plants to harvesting them responsibly and, of course, cooking up some delicious recipes.

As we dive into the world of foraging in Texas, we'll start by exploring the state's different regions. Each area has unique weather patterns and land-scapes, which play a huge role in the types of plants you'll find. You'll learn about the different types of plants that grow in each region and get to know some of the most popular wild edibles you can find.

But it's not just about the plants themselves – it's about the experience, too! Foraging is an awesome way to connect with nature and enjoy some fresh air. Plus, knowing you've found and prepared your meal with your hands is super satisfying. Trust us – there's nothing quite like the taste of a meal made from wild edibles you've foraged yourself.

We'll introduce you to local foraging groups and resources throughout the book. These communities are full of passionate people who love to share their knowledge and experiences with others. Joining a foraging group is an excellent way to learn, make new friends, and explore the great outdoors together. Who knows, you might even discover some hidden gems right in your backyard!

And let's not forget the recipes! After all, the best part of foraging is tasting the incredible flavors of the plants you've found. We'll share some delicious, easy-to-follow recipes that showcase the best of Texas' wild edibles. From prickly pear cactus to morel mushrooms, you'll be cooking up a storm in no time.

So, are you ready to embark on this wild adventure? We promise you that it's going to be a fun, exciting, and delicious experience. With this guide by your side, you'll discover a whole new world of flavors and connect with the natural beauty of the Lone Star State.

Let's begin this fantastic journey, and together, we'll explore the wonderful world of foraging in Texas. Here's to countless adventures, new friendships, and mouthwatering meals from Texas's wild and beautiful plants. Happy foraging, y'all!

PART ONE
TEXAS
A FLAVORFUL FORAY THROUGH THE LONE STAR STATE'S DIVERSE REGIONS

CHAPTER 1
DISCOVER CENTRAL TEXAS
A WONDERLAND OF NATURAL BEAUTY, HISTORY, AND ADVENTURE

Welcome to Central Texas, a region known for its rolling hills, vibrant wildflowers, and rich cultural history that spans generations. From the bustling city of Austin to the tranquil beauty of Hill Country, Central Texas has something to offer everyone, whether you're a nature lover, a history buff, or simply looking for a fun-filled getaway.

Yearly Weather Patterns and Land Topography

- **Winter (December - February):** Cool and mild, with average temperatures ranging from 40°F to 60°F. Occasional cold snaps and light snowfall.
- **Spring (March - May):** Mild and pleasant, with temperatures ranging from 60°F to 80°F. Wildflowers in full bloom, with bluebonnets stealing the show.
- **Summer (June - August):** Hot and humid, with average temperatures reaching 90°F to 100°F. Occasional thunderstorms and drought conditions.
- **Fall (September - November):** Warm and mild, with temperatures ranging from 60°F to 80°F. Fall foliage adds vibrant colors to the landscape.

Central Texas boasts a diverse topography with the following key features:

- Rolling hills and plateaus, particularly in the Texas Hill Country

- Limestone cliffs and caves provide habitats for numerous species
- Riparian ecosystems along the Colorado, Brazos, and Guadalupe Rivers
- Expansive grasslands and prairies, home to various native plants and wildlife

---

"You may all go to hell, and I will go to Texas."

- DAVY CROCKETT

There's no denying that the Lone Star State has always held a special allure for those seeking adventure and a connection to the great outdoors.

Hotspots in Central Texas

Central Texas offers many opportunities for enthusiasts to explore and connect with nature. Here are a few popular areas of interest:

- **Balcones Canyonlands National Wildlife Refuge:** An expansive natural area with diverse habitats, perfect for discovering wild edibles and native plants.
- **McKinney Falls State Park:** A picturesque park with waterfalls, creeks, and plenty of trails to explore while foraging native plants and mushrooms.
- **Pedernales Falls State Park:** Featuring the beautiful Pedernales River, this park offers a mix of forest, grasslands, and riverbanks to search for wild edibles.
- **Enchanted Rock State Natural Area:** A massive pink granite dome with surrounding forests and creeks, ideal for foraging adventures.

Local Foraging Groups and Resources

Interested in joining a community of fellow foragers? Here are some Central Texas-based groups and resources to help you get started:

- **Austin Wild Foods & Foraging:** A meetup group organizes foraging walks, workshops, and events. https://www.meetup.com/Austin-Wild-Foods-Foraging/
- **Texas Master Naturalist Program:** Offers training and volunteer opportunities for individuals interested in learning about and conserving Texas' natural resources. https://txmn.org/

- **Central Texas Mycological Society:** A group dedicated to the study and appreciation of fungi, with a focus on Central Texas species. https://centraltexasmycology.org/

As you venture deeper into the heart of Texas, you'll soon discover Central Texas is just the beginning of your foraging journey. Next, we'll explore the lush forests, swamps, and bayous of East Texas, where a treasure trove of wild edibles and fascinating ecosystems awaits. Are you ready to take on the challenge and uncover the hidden gems of the Lone Star?

CHAPTER 2
EXPLORING EAST TEXAS
A FORAGER'S PARADISE

As we continue our journey through Texas, we now find ourselves in the eastern part of the state, a region characterized by dense forests, swamps, bayous, and a wide variety of plant and animal life. East Texas is a forager's paradise, with countless opportunities to discover new flavors, learn about the natural world, and immerse yourself in the region's unique beauty.

Yearly Weather Patterns and Land Topography

- **Winter (December - February):** Cool and wet, with average temperatures ranging from 40°F to 60°F. Rare instances of snow and ice.
- **Spring (March - May):** Warm and humid, with temperatures ranging from 60°F to 80°F. Springtime brings stunning displays of flowering dogwoods, azaleas, and other native plants.
- **Summer (June - August):** Hot and humid, with average temperatures around 80°F to 95°F. Afternoon thunderstorms are common.
- **Fall (September - November):** Mild and pleasant, with temperatures ranging from 55°F to 80°F. Fall foliage adds a colorful backdrop to the region's forests.

East Texas is known for its diverse landscapes, including:

- **Pineywoods:** Vast expanses of pine and hardwood forests, teeming with wildlife and plant species
- **Big Thicket:** A unique blend of ecosystems, including swamps, bayous, and forests, home to numerous rare and endangered species
- **Riverine ecosystems:** The Sabine, Neches, and Trinity Rivers provide fertile habitats for various plants and animals.

"East Texas is not without its man-made curiosities, but it is the natural world that has given the region its identity."

- JOE R. LANSDALE, AN EAST TEXAS-BASED AUTHOR, AND WRITER

Hotspots in East Texas

There's no shortage of opportunities in East Texas. Here are some popular destinations for nature enthusiasts:

- **Big Thicket National Preserve:** A biodiverse wonderland perfect for discovering a variety of wild edibles, from mushrooms to native plants.
- **Caddo Lake State Park:** Explore the mysterious beauty of Caddo Lake and its surrounding bayous and swamps, home to numerous wild edibles.
- **Davy Crockett National Forest:** A stunning forested area with abundant foraging opportunities amidst towering pines and hardwoods.
- **Martin Creek Lake State Park:** Wander along the shores of Martin Creek Lake, where you'll find a variety of wild edibles, from berries to mushrooms.

Local Foraging Groups and Resources

Connect with fellow foragers and deepen your understanding of East Texas' natural bounty with these local groups and resources:

- **East Texas Foragers:** A Facebook group dedicated to sharing knowledge, tips, and experiences related to foraging in East Texas. https://www.facebook.com/groups/1567658343408915/

- **Native Plant Society of Texas:** A statewide organization focused on conserving Texas' native plants and habitats, with local chapters throughout the state. https://npsot.org/wp/
- **East Texas Mycological Society:** A group for mushroom enthusiasts in East Texas, offering workshops, events, and identification assistance. https://www.facebook.com/EastTexasMycologicalSociety/

East Texas is a true forager's paradise just waiting to be discovered. So gather your basket and sense of adventure, and embark on a journey through the captivating landscapes of the Lone Star State while we continue our trip to South Texas.

CHAPTER 3
JOURNEY TO SOUTH TEXAS
A TAPESTRY OF CULTURES, FLAVORS, AND NATURAL BEAUTY

South Texas is steeped in history, culture, and breathtaking landscapes. From the sun-soaked shores of the Gulf Coast to the rugged beauty of the South Texas Plains, you'll find a fascinating tapestry of flavors, wildlife, and natural wonders that beckon to be explored.

Yearly Weather Patterns and Land Topography

- **Winter (December - February):** Mild and cool, with average temperatures ranging from 50°F to 70°F. Occasional cold snaps and light frost.
- **Spring (March - May):** Warm and humid, with temperatures ranging from 70°F to 85°F. Wildflowers and blooming cacti paint the landscape.
- **Summer (June - August):** Hot and humid, with average temperatures hovering around 90°F to 100°F. Frequent afternoon thunderstorms and high humidity.
- **Fall (September - November):** Warm and mild, with temperatures ranging from 70°F to 85°F. Coastal breezes provide relief from the heat.

South Texas offers a diverse range of landforms, including:

- **Gulf Coast:** Sandy beaches, coastal marshes, and tidal flats teeming with marine life

- **Rio Grande Valley:** Fertile river deltas, subtropical forests, and agricultural lands
- **South Texas Plains:** Expansive grasslands, thorn scrub, and oak savannas, home to numerous species of plants and animals

---

"Texas is a state of mind. Texas is an obsession. Above all, Texas is a nation in every sense of the word."

JOHN STEINBECK, AMERICAN AUTHOR

Indeed, South Texas embodies the spirit of the Lone Star State with its rich history, unique flavors, and stunning landscapes.

Hotspots in South Texas

South Texas is home to a variety of ecosystems that provide ample opportunities. Here are a few popular areas of interest:

- **Padre Island National Seashore:** Discover edible coastal plants and marine life along the pristine beaches of this barrier island.
- **Laguna Atascosa National Wildlife Refuge:** Explore diverse habitats, from tidal marshes to thorn forests, in search of native plants and wild edibles.
- **Falcon State Park:** Wander through the arid South Texas Plains, foraging for cacti, yucca, and other desert-adapted plants.
- **Estero Llano Grande State Park:** Search for wild edibles among the subtropical woodlands and wetlands of this Rio Grande Valley gem.

Local Foraging Groups and Resources

Connect with like-minded individuals and expand your knowledge of South Texas' natural bounty through these local foraging groups and resources:

- **South Texas Foraging Enthusiasts:** A Facebook group dedicated to sharing tips, recipes, and experiences related to foraging in South Texas. https://www.facebook.com/groups/1567658343408915/
- **Rio Grande Valley Chapter of the Native Plant Society of Texas:** A local chapter of a statewide organization focused on conserving native plants and habitats. https://npsot.org/wp/rgv/
- **Coastal Bend Mycological Society:** A group that promotes the study and enjoyment of fungi, focusing on species found in the South Texas

Coastal Bend region. https://www.facebook.com/CoastalBendMyco
logicalSociety/

As we leave the sun-kissed shores and rich cultural tapestry of South Texas behind, we now set our sights on West Texas's rugged, untamed beauty. From the vast expanses of the Chihuahuan Desert to the majestic peaks of the Guadalupe Mountains, West Texas offers a whole new world of foraging adventures and breathtaking landscapes. Join us as we venture further into the heart of the Lone Star State, uncovering this beautiful region's unique flavors, natural wonders, and timeless allure.

CHAPTER 4
SEE WEST TEXAS
A LAND OF CONTRASTS, MYSTERY, AND UNPARALLELED BEAUTY

Welcome to West Texas, a region defined by its striking contrasts, stark beauty, and endless horizons. From the sprawling Chihuahuan Desert to the majestic Guadalupe Mountains, West Texas is a land of extremes that invites you to explore its hidden treasures, unearth its ancient history, and embrace its untamed spirit.

Yearly Weather Patterns and Land Topography

- **Winter (December-February):** Cold and dry, with average temperatures ranging from 30°F to 60°F. Occasional snowfall, especially in mountainous areas.
- **Spring (March-May):** Mild and windy, with temperatures ranging from 50°F to 80°F. Wildflowers and blooming cacti add color to the desert landscape.
- **Summer (June-August):** Hot and dry, with average temperatures between 85°F and 100°F. Brief afternoon thunderstorms may bring relief from the heat.
- **Fall (September-November):** Warm and mild, with temperatures ranging from 50°F to 80°F. Crisp nights and clear skies make for excellent stargazing.

West Texas is known for its diverse and striking landscapes, including:

- **Chihuahuan Desert:** A vast expanse of arid scrublands, home to unique flora and fauna

- **Davis Mountains:** A sky island mountain range featuring lush forests, meadows, and a wide variety of plant life
- **Guadalupe Mountains:** The highest peaks in Texas, with diverse habitats ranging from desert lowlands to lush alpine forests
- **Big Bend Country:** A remote and rugged region where the Rio Grande has carved dramatic canyons and valleys

---

"Texas is not just a state. It's a state of mind. It's a sense of place."

- ANN RICHARDS, FORMER TEXAS GOVERNOR

West Texas embodies this sentiment with its stark beauty, boundless skies, and rugged landscapes that inspire a sense of wonder and adventure.

Hotspots in West Texas

Though West Texas may seem barren at first glance, it holds a wealth of opportunities for those willing to explore its unique landscapes. Here are a few popular areas of interest:

- **Big Bend National Park:** Forage for edible desert plants and marvel at the awe-inspiring beauty of the Chisos Mountains and Rio Grande canyons.
- **Guadalupe Mountains National Park:** Discover a variety of wild edibles, from prickly pear cactus to mountain mahogany, as you explore the highest peaks in Texas.
- **Davis Mountains State Park:** Wander through lush forests and meadows, searching for wild mushrooms, berries, and native plants.
- **Franklin Mountains State Park:** Explore the rugged desert landscape, foraging for desert-adapted plants like yucca, agave, and mesquite.

Local Foraging Groups and Resources

Expand your knowledge of West Texas' natural bounty and connect with fellow foragers through these local groups and resources:

- **West Texas Foragers:** A Facebook group where members share their foraging experiences, tips, and recipes focused on West Texas. https://www.facebook.com/groups/westtexasforagers/

- **Trans-Pecos Chapter of the Native Plant Society of Texas:** A local chapter dedicated to the conservation and study of native plants and habitats in the Trans-Pecos region. https://npsot.org/wp/trans-pecos/
- **Texas Mushroom Identification:** A group for mushroom enthusiasts in Texas that offers identification assistance. Facebook Page: Facebook Page

We hope you've enjoyed exploring West Texas's rugged, mysterious beauty as we conclude our journey through the Lone Star State. From the vast Chihuahuan Desert to the majestic Guadalupe Mountains, this captivating region offers a wealth of foraging opportunities, natural wonders, and unforgettable experiences. With its diverse landscapes, unique flavors, and boundless skies, West Texas will surely leave a lasting impression on your heart and inspire a lifelong love for the great outdoors.

PART TWO
LEARNING CURVE
THE BASICS OF FORAGING

CHAPTER 5
FORAGING 101
A BEGINNER'S GUIDE TO UNEARTHING NATURE'S CULINARY TREASURES

Welcome to the fantastic world of foraging! If you're here, it probably means you're curious about exploring the great outdoors and discovering nature's delicious treasures. And you're not alone – foraging is becoming more and more popular as people look for fun, eco-friendly, and healthy ways to enjoy their food. So, get ready to embark on a thrilling adventure as we dive into the basics of foraging!

Foraging is all about finding, harvesting, and enjoying wild plants that grow naturally around us. It's an age-old practice that our ancestors relied on for their food and medicine. But don't worry; you don't need to be a survival expert to try foraging. With a little bit of knowledge and guidance, anyone can learn how to spot tasty wild edibles and whip up a delicious meal with their finds.

Before we jump into the nitty-gritty of foraging, let's talk about some of the great reasons why people love this unique hobby:

1 Connecting with nature: Foraging is a fantastic way to spend time outdoors and develop a deeper appreciation for the environment. You'll learn to see the world around you in a new light as you discover the incredible plants growing in your area.

2 Trying new flavors: Wild edibles can add a whole new dimension to your meals with flavors you won't find at the grocery store. Plus, you'll get to impress your friends and family with your culinary creations.

3 Health benefits: Many wild plants are packed with nutrients, making them a healthy addition to your diet. Foraging also involves plenty of walking, bending, and stretching – a fun way to sneak in some exercise!

4 Saving money: Foraging can help you cut your grocery bills since you'll be sourcing some food for free. Plus, you might even stumble upon some rare and expensive ingredients, like morel mushrooms or wild truffles.

Now that you know why foraging is so amazing, let's talk about some of the basics you'll need to keep in mind as you start your foraging journey:

Safety first: When it comes to foraging, safety is the number one priority. You'll need to learn to identify plants accurately, as some wild edibles have poisonous look-alikes. Start by familiarizing yourself with common edible plants in your area and their toxic counterparts. Invest in a good field guide or take a class with a local expert to help build your confidence.

Dress for success: When you head out for a foraging expedition, you'll want to dress appropriately for the occasion. Wear sturdy shoes, long pants, and sleeves to protect yourself from thorns, insects, and poison ivy. A hat and sunscreen are also a must to shield yourself from the sun.

Pack your gear: A few essential tools can make your foraging experience much more enjoyable. Bring a basket or bag to carry your finds, a sharp knife or pair of scissors for cutting plants, and a field guide or smartphone app to help with identification. And don't forget to pack some water and snacks to keep you energized!

Get creative in the kitchen: Once you've gathered your wild edibles, it's time to have some fun in the kitchen. Experiment with new recipes and cooking techniques to maximize your foraged ingredients. From salads and soups to teas and desserts, the possibilities are endless!

So, now that we've covered the basics, it's time to start thinking about where to begin your foraging adventures. Start by exploring your local area – you might be surprised by the abundance of wild edibles growing right in your backyard or at a nearby park. As you gain experience and confidence, you can venture out to more diverse habitats like forests, meadows, and even beaches.

One of the best ways to learn about foraging is by connecting with others who share your passion. Look for local foraging groups, workshops, or classes where you can meet experienced foragers and learn from their exper-tise. These communities are a goldmine of information and support, and you'll likely make new friends along the way.

Patience and curiosity are your best allies when it comes to foraging. You'll likely encounter some challenges as you learn to identify plants and navigate different terrains but don't get discouraged. With time and practice, you'll develop a keen eye for spotting wild edibles and a wealth of knowledge about the plants that grow around you.

Remember, foraging is meant to be fun, engaging, and rewarding. Embrace the process of learning and discovery, and don't be afraid to make mistakes. The more time you spend outdoors, the more in tune you'll become with the rhythms of nature and the bountiful treasures it has to offer.

In conclusion, foraging is an incredible hobby that allows you to connect with nature, discover new flavors, and enjoy the satisfaction of sourcing your food. As you embark on this exciting journey, remember to prioritize safety, practice sustainable harvesting, and embrace the spirit of adventure.

With a bit of patience, curiosity, and a sense of wonder, you'll unlock the secrets of the wild edibles around you and open up a whole new world of culinary possibilities. So, go ahead and step into the great outdoors – a delicious, nature-filled adventure awaits! Happy foraging!

CHAPTER 6

A RESPONSIBLE APPROACH TO HARVESTING NATURE'S GIFTS

ETHICAL AND SUSTAINABLE FORAGING

Welcome, fellow foragers! As we embark on our exciting journey to discover the wild edibles of Texas, it's essential to remember that our actions impact the environment around us. By practicing ethical and sustainable foraging, we can enjoy the delicious and nutritious bounty of nature while also protecting and preserving the ecosystems we love. In this chapter, we'll explore the principles of responsible foraging, from understanding local rules and regulations to cultivating a deep connection with the land.

Follow the Rules and Regulations

The first step in ethical foraging is knowing and respecting the laws and guidelines governing wild plant collection. Different parks, nature reserves, and public lands may have specific regulations regarding foraging, so be sure to research the rules before you head out. Some areas may require permits or limit the number of certain species you can harvest, while others may prohibit foraging altogether. By following these rules, we can protect the environment and ensure that future generations can enjoy the pleasures of foraging.

Harvest Responsibly

When collecting wild edibles, a little restraint goes a long way. Always practice the "rule of thirds" when harvesting: take only a third of what you find, leave a third for wildlife, and leave the remaining third for the plants to regenerate. Be sure to use clean, sharp tools to minimize damage and avoid harvesting immature plants or those that appear stressed or diseased.

Remember, we're not just foraging for ourselves but also acting as stewards of the land.

Leave No Trace

As foragers, we should always strive to leave the environment in better condition than we found it. Practice the "Leave No Trace" principles by staying on designated trails, packing out trash, and minimizing your impact on the natural world. By leaving no trace of our presence, we can help preserve the beauty and integrity of the land for years to come.

Habitat and Life Cycle of the Plants

Understanding the habitat and life cycle of the plants you're foraging is crucial for sustainable harvesting. By studying the environmental conditions specific plants need to thrive, you can ensure that you're not disrupting the ecosystem or causing harm. Be mindful of the seasonality of plants and only harvest when they're at their peak, as this ensures a higher quality of food and minimizes the impact on the plant population.

Monitor and Learn from Your Impact

Ethical foraging is a continuous learning process. As you become more familiar with the plants you harvest, note how your actions affect the environment. Are the plants regenerating well after you've gathered them? Are you noticing any changes in the local ecosystem? By observing and learning from your impact, you can adapt your foraging practices to be more sustainable and environmentally friendly.

Share Your Knowledge and Passion

One of the most powerful ways to promote sustainable foraging is by sharing your knowledge and passion with others. Teach your friends and family about responsible harvesting practices and preserving the environment. By spreading the word, we can help foster a community of ethical foragers dedicated to protecting our natural world.

Embrace the Principles of Permaculture and Regenerative Harvesting

Ethical foraging goes hand-in-hand with permaculture and regenerative harvesting principles. These practices emphasize working with nature rather than against it and focus on creating abundant, self-sustaining ecosystems. By incorporating these ideas into our foraging, we can support the health and well-being of the land while still enjoying its delicious gifts.

Cultivate Gratitude and Reverence for Nature

Lastly, ethical foraging is rooted in a deep sense of gratitude and reverence for nature. As we explore the wild edibles of Texas, let's take a moment to appreciate the incredible abundance and beauty of the land. By cultivating gratitude, we can develop a deeper connection with the environment and become more mindful of our actions.

Ethical and sustainable foraging is not just about finding tasty morsels in the wild but also about fostering a harmonious relationship with nature. So, as you venture out into the beautiful landscapes of Texas, keep these principles in mind and remember that we are all part of a larger ecosystem. Practicing ethical foraging can help protect the environment, support biodiversity, and make a positive difference in the world. Happy foraging, and may your adventures be filled with delicious discoveries and a profound appreciation for the wonders of nature!

NOTE FROM THE PUBLISHER:

Note from the Publisher: *We completely understand the advantages of using color photos to identify plants. However, to make this book edition more affordable, we decided to use black and white photographs, which helped us reduce printing costs, and we passed those savings on to you. But don't worry, we have a solution for you! Scan the QR code below and download a complimentary printable PDF file that includes vibrant, clear, color photos of all the plants featured in the book. Happy Foraging!*

The stars at night are big and bright
Deep in the heart of Texas
The prairie sky is wide and high
Deep in the heart of Texas

The sage in bloom is like perfume
Deep in the heart of Texas
Reminds me of the one that I love
Deep in the heart of Texas

— JUNE HERSHEY

PART THREE
EASING INTO EDIBLE PLANTS
FUN AND SAFE WILD EDIBLES FOR THE WHOLE FAMILY

This part of the book is all about discovering the incredible world of foraging with your loved ones. We'll be guiding you through the process of finding, identifying, and enjoying some of the safest and most delicious wild edibles that nature has to offer. So gather up the kids, grab your foraging gear, and let's embark on a family adventure that's fun, educational, and oh-so-tasty!

One of the most rewarding aspects of foraging is the opportunity to share your passion for nature with your family. As you explore the great outdoors, your kids will develop a deep appreciation for the environment, learn essential life skills, and make lasting memories that they'll treasure forever. Plus, there's nothing quite like the thrill of discovering a patch of juicy berries or a cluster of delectable mushrooms hidden in the underbrush!

Before diving into the world of family-friendly foraging, let's cover a few basics to ensure that your adventures are safe and enjoyable. First and foremost, it's essential to remember that not all plants are created equal. Some wild edibles can look strikingly similar to their toxic counterparts, so it's crucial to become familiar with the plants you're seeking before heading out. In this part of the book, we've carefully selected plants that are both safe to consume and relatively easy to identify, giving you peace of mind as you forage with your family.

Next, be sure to pack the right gear for your foraging expeditions. Comfortable clothes, sturdy shoes, and sun protection are must-haves for every adventure. It's also a good idea to bring along a field guide, a basket or bag for collecting your finds, and a small knife or pair of scissors for snipping off leaves, stems, and fruit. Don't forget to pack plenty of water and snacks, too – foraging can be hard work!

As you begin your foraging journey, you'll quickly discover that the world of wild edibles is vast and diverse. From sun-kissed meadows to shady forests, there are countless habitats just waiting to be explored. In this part of the book, we'll introduce you to a variety of family-friendly plants that can be found in various environments across the United States. Some examples include:

• Juicy wild berries like blackberries, raspberries, and mulberries

• Tasty tree nuts such as acorns, walnuts, and pecans

• Delightful greens like dandelion leaves, purslane, and lamb's quarters

As you encounter these wild edibles and more, encourage your kids to use all of their senses to truly appreciate the plants they're discovering. Touch the leaves, smell the flowers, and (once you're sure of their identity) taste the fruit. This sensory exploration will not only make foraging more fun, but it will also help your children develop a deeper understanding of the plants they're encountering.

Finally, remember that foraging is all about enjoying nature and spending quality time with your family. Don't be discouraged if you don't find a bumper crop of wild edibles on your first outing – the joy of foraging lies in the journey, not just the destination. Take the time to appreciate the beauty of your surroundings and the company of your loved ones. Before you know it, you'll be making priceless memories and forging a family bond that's rooted in the wonders of the natural world.

So, are you ready to embark on a foraging adventure that's as fun as it is delicious? Grab your loved ones, lace up your hiking boots, and let's head out into the wild – the world of family-friendly foraging awaits!

Sugar Hackberry
Celtis laevigata [SEL-TIS LEE-VI-GAH-TUH]

This tree is a member of the Cannabaceae family and goes by several other names, including Celtis laevigata, Sugarberry, and Southern Hackberry. Initially, this tree was valued for its hardy wood, which was used to create a variety of tools, furniture, and even wagons.

Location: Sugar Hackberry is native to Texas and can be found in the state's eastern, central, and southern regions. It thrives in a variety of habitats, including floodplains, riverbanks, and moist, well-drained soils.

Identification:

GROWTH / SIZE: A medium to large deciduous tree, growing between 30 and 70 feet tall with a trunk diameter of 1 to 3 feet.

BARK / STEM / ROOT: The bark is light gray and often has warty, corky ridges. Its branches are slender, and the roots are shallow and spreading, making it well-suited for growing in various soil types.

Leaf: The leaves are simple, alternate, and ovate to lanceolate in shape, measuring 2 to 4 inches long and 1 to 2 inches wide. The leaves are dark green on top and pale green underneath, with slightly serrated edges.

Flower: The tree produces small, greenish-white flowers that are typically inconspicuous. They bloom in the spring, usually from March to April.

Fruit/Seed/Nut: Sugar Hackberry produces small, round, sweet drupes that are about 1/4 inch in diameter. When ripe, these fruits turn from green to a dark purple or black color and contain a single, hard seed.

Look-A-Like Plants: Sugar Hackberry can be confused with other hackberry species, such as the **Common Hackberry** (*Celtis occidentalis*). However, these trees are not toxic and can be distinguished by examining their leaves, bark, and fruit.

Cautions: There are no significant cautions associated with Sugar Hackberry.

Culinary Preparations: The sweet fruits are edible and can be consumed raw or used to make jams, jellies, and preserves. Native Americans also ground the seeds to create nutritious flour.

Medicinal Uses: Traditionally, it was used by Native Americans to treat various ailments, such as sore throats, coughs, and digestive issues. However, modern research on the medicinal properties of this tree is limited.

Fun or Historical Fact: Sugar Hackberry trees provide essential habitat and food for various wildlife species, including birds, squirrels, and deer. The sweet fruits are particularly attractive to birds, which help disperse the seeds and contribute to the tree's propagation.

Dog Toxicity: Sugar Hackberry is not known to be toxic to dogs. However, as with any plant, it is essential to prevent your dog from ingesting large quantities to avoid potential gastrointestinal upset. If your dog shows symptoms like vomiting, diarrhea, or loss of appetite after consuming parts of the tree, consult your veterinarian for advice.

Chickweed

Stellaria media [STELL-AR-ee-uh MEED-ee-uh]

Chickweed grows everywhere, which is excellent news for foragers because it's almost as tasty as it is nutritious. It's also effortless to harvest. It's part of the *Caryophyllaceae* (carnation) family and has multiple names, such as starweed, Birdweed, Chickenwort, Starweed, Starwort, Winterweed, and mouse ear.

Locate: Chickweed grows almost everywhere, including backyards, parks, grasslands, fields, and wastelands.

Identify:

GROWTH/SIZE - It grows in large patches, forming mats that can grow to 1-2 feet tall and round.

BARK/STEM - The succulent stems are green or burgundy and often have white hairs.

Leaf - The leaves are **oval-ovate**, to broadly **elliptic** along their margins, hairless on top, and occasionally hairy on the bottom. The stems at the bottom of the plant have short, hairy **petioles**, while the leaves near the tip are **sessile**. They are more prominent at the ends of the stems, spanning up to ¾ inch in length and ½ inch across.

Flower - There are white, small flowers with distinctly lobed petals. In most cases, there are three stamens and three styles. The flowers don't take long to form capsules; a plant can have both flowers and capsules.

Fruit/seed - Seed capsules replace each flower; they're light brown, with six small teeth along their upper rim and several seeds. Mature seeds are reddish brown, slightly flattened, and orbicular-reniform; they have minute bumps on their surface.

Look-a-likes: One toxic look-alike is the scarlet pimpernel. You can tell the difference by looking for the line of fine hairs along the stem, as the scarlet pimpernel doesn't have it. The flowers are also reddish-orange, and the plant itself has milky sap.

Caution: Nausea, upset stomach, diarrhea, and vomiting can result from too much chickweed.

Prepare: You can eat chickweed raw in salads or use it to make pestos or green smoothies. Chickweed will keep in the fridge for a few days if you wrap it in a damp paper towel and put it in a plastic bag. It also freezes reasonably well if you blend it up first.

Medicinal Info/Use: Soothing, cooling, hydrating, and healing, chickweed has it all. For skin inflammation, wounds, boils, rashes, acne, and drawing out infections. It's applied topically as a plant poultice or infused in olive oil. Our ability to absorb nutrients improves when we eat chickweed. Combining this with the high fiber and mineral content makes chickweed a highly effective digestive support aid.

Fun Fact: Chickweed makes excellent food for poultry as well.

Pet Toxicity: Chickweed is not toxic for dogs; quite the opposite. There are several uses for chickweed when it comes to your best friend.

- **Hotspots and Skin irritation:** make a poultice using chickweed to soothe the burns, hotspots, and skin irritations.
- **Tinctures:** used as an astringent to help clean and heal minor skin wounds by applying juice fresh from the stem.
- **Tea:** because it's tasty and easy for pups to digest, it can be used to soothe the occasional upset stomach.

C hicory

Cichorium intybus [sɪk-KOR-ee-um IN-tye-bus]

Chicory is incredibly common, and once you know what to look for, you'll probably find it everywhere. It belongs to the *Asteraceae* (daisy) family. It is known by several names, such as blue daisy, blue dandelion, blue sailors, blueweed, coffee weed, cornflower, horseweed, and wild endive.

Locate: Chicory grows readily in disturbed areas, like wastelands, meadows, fields, and roadsides.

Identify:

Growth/Size - This biennial plant grows from two to four feet tall and one foot wide.

Bark/Stem - It has erect green or reddish-brown stems with a fleshy taproot that exudes a milky sap when cut.

Leaf - Generally, **alternate** leaves are up to eight inches long and two inches wide, becoming smaller as they ascend the stem. These leaves are *lance-*

shaped and resemble dandelion leaves at the base. The leaves gradually narrow where they are *sessile* or clasp the stem. Depending on where the leaves are on the branch, they have lobed edges, dentate edges, or they lose their *petioles* and hold the stem. In the lower leaf surface, the central vein usually has many hairs.

FLOWER - With numerous bright blue rays and blunt-toothed edges, these flowers have *ligulate flower heads* up to 1.5 inches long. These flowers have no stalks and grow along stems, opening up in the morning and closing up by noon unless it's cloudy, appearing from mid-summer until the first frost.

FRUIT/SEED - Has *achene* with a brown oval shape, five ribs, and blunt ends. On the broader end, there are bristles across the top.

Look-a-likes: Chicory plants are distinctive with their flowers and have no toxic relatives. Only dandelions and daisies are easier to identify among wildflowers for a beginner forager.

Caution: Chicory might have been sprayed with herbicides as it's considered a weed. Avoid harvesting chicory that's too close to busy roads.

Prepare: The leaves and flowers are bitter and can be used in salads. Use sparingly and, if need be, blanch the leaves to take away some of the bitterness. In addition, chicory roots can also be roasted, ground, or blended with coffee to make a less expensive and caffeine-free beverage.

Medicinal Info/Use: In the laboratory, root extracts have also been shown to be antibacterial, anti-inflammatory, and mildly sedative. In addition, they slow down and weaken the pulse, as well as lower blood sugar levels. Extracts from leaves have similar effects, though they are weaker. To treat swellings, bruised leaves were used as a poultice. A root extract can treat fevers and jaundice, as well as as a diuretic and laxative.

Fun Fact: You can spot chicory by looking for distinctive blueish-purple flowers. Initially brought to the United States by the colonists as a medicinal herb, chicory was cultivated by Thomas Jefferson and others as a forage crop. As it does not dry well, horses, cattle, sheep, poultry, and rabbits were usually fed it fresh.

Home Gardens: If edible gardening is what you are looking for, then this one is for you. It's a fairly hardy plant and is drought resistant, but it also attracts bees and butterflies, so it will help pollinate the rest of your garden.

Pet Toxicity: Chicory is pet safe and can benefit your pet's health.

D andelion
Taraxacum officinale [ta-RAKS-uh-kum oh-fiss-ih-NAH-lee]

Dandelions are one of the most common edibles and are found all over the world. They're easy to spot, which makes them a fantastic foraging option for beginners. They belong to the **Asteraceae** (daisy) family and have only one different name: Lion's tooth.

Locate: Dandelions prefer shady, cooler areas, but you'll also find them in direct sunlight. To the distaste of many homeowners, they grow on lawns. Potential habitats include parks, pastures, orchards, hayfields, meadows, and disturbed areas such as roadsides and wastelands.

Identify:

GROWTH/SIZE - You can quickly identify Dandelions by their distinctive yellow blooms. It is a fast-spreading broadleaf perennial weed that spreads by seed. The plant grows 2-6 inches tall and can get as wide as 2 feet.

Bark/Stem - Leafless and unbranched hollow stems form deep taproots, and milky latex sap flows throughout the plant.

Leaf - A **basal rosette** is formed in an **oblanceolate** shape. Deeply toothed, backward-pointing teeth or lobes are present on rosette leaves at the base.

Flower - A bright yellow ray flower with toothed tips appears throughout the year on second-year plants. In the evening, they close their petals, which are single heads on their stems.

Fruit/seed - Seed heads are fluffy, round, downy, and dispersed by the wind.

Look-a-likes: Cat's Ear (*Hypochaeris radicata*) is the most likely to be mistaken for dandelion, as the flower heads look very similar. Cat's Ear does not have hollow stems, and their stems are branching. They also have hairy leaves with deep notches.

Sow Thistle (*Sonchus spp.*) also does not have hollow stems, and the leaves grow up the entire stalk with multiple flowers growing from each branch. In the thistle family, the mature plant also has prickly spines.

Caution: None plant-related, but be sure to check if they have been sprayed with a weed killer before eating.

Prepare: The entire dandelion plant is edible, but you must prepare the greens and the root differently. The greens can be eaten raw or added to salads, they have an earthy and bitter taste, and it's best to use young leaves. The leaves can also be sautéed in olive oil and garlic and seasoned. Flowers can be used to make dandelion wine, syrups, or even battered and fried like zucchini blossoms. Chopping and roasting the roots can be used to create tea.

Medicinal Info/Use: The dandelion is a commonly used herbal remedy. It is especially effective and valuable as a diuretic because it contains high levels of potassium salts and can replace the potassium lost from the body when used. The plant is used internally to treat gall bladder and urinary disorders, gallstones, jaundice, cirrhosis, dyspepsia with constipation, edema associated with high blood pressure and heart weakness, chronic joint and skin complaints, gout, eczema, and acne. The latex contained in the plant sap can be used to remove corn, warts, and verrucae.

Fun Fact: The yellow flowers can be dried and ground into a yellow-pigmented powder and used as a dye.

Home Gardens: Though considered a weed by most, they make an excellent addition to an edible garden. They will attract bees and other pollinators.

Pet Toxicity: Dandelion, though not toxic, can cause constipation and gas in some dogs. The dandelion will boost its immune system and help improve digestion. It also aids in building strong bones and teeth.

M allow
Malva neglecta [MAL-ᴠᴜʜ ɴᴇ-GLEK-ᴛᴜʜ]

Mallow is highly nutritious. For centuries, it has been used as food and for medicinal purposes. It belongs to the Malvaceae (mallow) family. Its other common names are Buttonweed, Creeping Charlie, Cheeseweed, high mallow, wood mallow, and dwarf mallow.

Locate: It grows on grassland, by roadsides, in a wasteland, with scrubs, cultivated gardens, and parks.

Identify: an *annual* or *biennial* invasive weed.

Gʀᴏᴡᴛʜ/Sɪᴢᴇ - The plant grows between 1-4 feet tall.

Bᴀʀᴋ/Sᴛᴇᴍ - It has a coarse, hairy stem that shoots off single ivy-like leaves.

Lᴇᴀꜰ - On the stem, the leaves are roundish, with numerous lobes, each 1 - 1 1/2 inches long, 1- 2 inches wide, and 2 to 4 inches in diameter. There are prominent veins on the leaf's underside and hairs radiating from a central point.

FLOWER - The flowers are reddish-purple, bright pinkish-purple with dark stripes, or bright mauve-purple with dark stripes. There are 2 to 4 axillary clusters along the main stem, with flowers at the base opening first. The flowers are in bloom from early Spring to early fall.

FRUIT/SEED - When ripe, the seeds are brown to brownish green, about 1/2 inch long, wide, and 1/3 inch across, and shaped like cheese wheels. Usually hairless, the nutlets have a sharp angle between the dorsal and lateral surfaces.

Look-a-likes: Common mallow can be confused with a common Carolina geranium. Geranium weed leaves, however, are more deeply divided.

Caution: The seeds can be toxic if eaten in large quantities but are otherwise safe and tasty.

Prepare: The seeds can be eaten raw as snacks. You can cook the leaves and prepare them like spinach or other greens. You can also eat or even pickle the flowers.

Medicinal Info/Use: In medieval herbal medicine, common mallow was used as a cure-all, like astringents, diuretics, emollients, expectorants, laxatives, and salves. The demulcent properties make it valuable as a poultice for bruises, inflammations, insect bites, etc. or ingested for respiratory and digestive problems. Combined with eucalyptus, it is a helpful remedy for coughs and other chest ailments.

Fun Fact: The original ingredient in marshmallows is Althaea officinalis or Marsh Mallow, one species in this family.

Home Gardens: Can be planted in an Edible garden.

Pet Toxicity: Low toxicity has been reported, but only when consumed in large quantities.

Purple Deadnettle

Lamium purpureum [LAY-mee-um pur-PUR-ee-um]

It is named for its leaves, which resemble stinging nettle (*Urtica*) but lack stings since they are "dead." It is a part of the **Lamiaceae** (mint or deadnettle) family and goes by these common names: Purple Archangel, Red Dead Nettle, and Velikdenche.

Locate: It prefers disturbed areas, such as footpaths, roadsides, and fields. It may even be in your backyard.

Identify: Purple dead nettle is an invaluable plant for pollinators. Its flowers attract bees and provide pollen that is an undyed red color.

GROWTH/SIZE - Can reach 8-10 inches tall.

BARK/STEM - Stems are square and green.

LEAF - Overlapping heart-shaped leaves are often purple, with greenish undersides and hairy upper surfaces. The leaf margins are wavy to serrated, and the petioles are short.

FLOWER - The purple flowers have a hooded top petal and two lips on the lower portion. Produced throughout the year, they are *sessile* and grow in *whorls* in the axils of the leaves.

FRUIT/SEED - A purple deadnettle plant produces 600 seeds but can have 27,000 when it's not competing with other plants for space.

Look-a-likes: It doesn't have any toxic look-a-likes, but in many places, it grows with Henbit Dead-nettle (*Lamium amplexicaule*), which is easily confused with purple deadnettle due to its similar leaves and bright purple flowers. Don't worry; they are both edible.

Caution: Those who eat generous amounts of dead nettle leaves may experience mild laxative effects. Consumption of too much herbal tea can cause diarrhea.

Prepare: The purple tops are slightly sweet, and the leaves are highly nutritious. It's usually used as a herb or garnish mixed with other greens.

Medicinal Info/Use: Purple deadnettle can be enjoyed internally and externally. It has been used for centuries to create salves, tinctures, and teas to treat various injuries or illnesses. It is an excellent source of vitamins A, C, and K, fiber, iron, and bioflavonoids. These leaves also have anti-inflammatory, antibacterial, and anti-fungal properties and are diuretic, astringent, diaphoretic, and purgative. Herbal remedies containing dead nettle have traditionally been used for treating kidney disease, seasonal allergies, chills, and common colds. In addition to boosting the immune system, consumption of this edible can also help combat bacterial infections. Additionally, the leaves can be used to create a poultice that can be used externally to heal cuts, burns, and bruises.

Fun Fact: Many myths and folklore stories surround this ancient plant. Traditionally, it has been used in magical ceremonies to promote happiness, security, and grounding. Those who wield this early-blooming plant are said to gain the same power it offers.

Home Gardens: can be added to an Edible garden and will attract bees and other pollinators.

Pet Toxicity: No evidence of toxicity or beneficial uses in pets exists.

P urslane

Portulaca oleracea [POR-TEW-LAK-UH AWL-LUR-RAY-SEE-UH]

Purslane is another weed that's common throughout North America and Eurasia. Some people deliberately cultivate it, but once you know how to spot it, you can quickly harvest it from the wild. It is a part of the Portulacaceae (purslane) family. It goes by these other names: Garden Purslane, Little Hogweed, Moss Rose, Pigweed, Portulaca, Red Root, Rock Moss, Verdolaga, and Wild Portulaca.

Locate: Purslane grows in wastelands and disturbed areas, such as gravelly soil and cracks in the sidewalk.

Identification:

GROWTH/SIZE - IT'S a low-growing, succulent annual plant that can grow up to 8 inches in height and 18 inches in width.

BARK/STEM /ROOT - The stem is fleshy and reddish-green, with a prostrate growth habit that produces many lateral branches. The roots are fibrous and shallow.

LEAF - The leaves are small, oval-shaped, ranging from 0.5 to 1.5 inches long. They are fleshy and succulent and range in color from green to red. The leaves grow alternately along the stem and have a smooth surface.

FLOWER - The flowers are small and cup-shaped, measuring approximately 0.5 to 0.75 inches in diameter. They are typically yellow but also pink, white, or red. The flowers bloom in the summer months and are produced in the axils of the leaves.

FRUIT/SEED/NUT - The fruit is a small capsule that contains many tiny, black seeds. The seeds are approximately 0.05 inches in diameter and are dispersed by wind and water. The plant also reproduces by rooting at the nodes of the stem, allowing it to spread rapidly and form dense mats on the ground.

Look-a-like(s): As mentioned before, spurges are the closest toxic look-alike to Purslane. The easiest way to tell the difference is to look for fleshy, succulent leaves. Spurges have flatter leaves and exude white latex when broken.

Caution: It may interact with certain medications, digestive upset, or allergic reactions.

Culinary Preparation: Immerse your collected Purslane in water to eliminate seeds and dirt. Get rid of thick stems and store them in the refrigerator. It has a mild, lemony flavor with a nice crunch. You can eat it raw in salads and sandwiches or steam it as a side dish. It also makes a delicious soup.

Medicinal Properties: It has been used for medicinal purposes for centuries in traditional Ayurveda, Chinese, and Unani cultures. Here are some traditional medicinal uses: anti-inflammatory properties due to the presence of flavonoids. It improves digestion and relieves constipation. Treats wounds, burns, and skin infections. It treats respiratory ailments such as asthma, coughs, and bronchitis. Its also used in modern medicine for its potential health benefits. Here are some of the contemporary medicinal uses of Portulaca oleracea: studies have shown that Portulaca oleracea may have anti-cancer effects, potentially due to its high antioxidant content and ability to inhibit cancer cell growth.

Fun Fact: It was a popular food among ancient Greeks and Romans, who believed it to have medicinal properties and ate it as a vegetable. The plant was also a common food source among Native Americans, who used it to make porridge or boil it as a green vegetable.

Dog Toxicity: Purslane is toxic to your pup and can cause a metabolic imbalance. Some signs of metabolic imbalance are hypersalivation, weakness, and tremors. If your dog exhibits these symptoms, it could be at risk for kidney failure.

A merican Beech

Fagus grandifolia [FAG-us GRAN-dih-FOH-lee-uh]

Beechnuts are sweet and delicious. The American Beech is a part of the Fagaceae (beech) family. Other common names for this tree include Beechnut Tree, Red Beech, Ridge Beech, and White Beech. In documented history, the oldest tree dates back 246 years.

Locate: Beech trees can be found in hardwood forests and prefers moist, well-drained soil. You can usually find them with maple trees.

Identification:

GROWTH/SIZE: The height of this large deciduous tree can range from 52 to 115 feet.

BARK/STEM/ROOT: Their bark is distinctively smooth, thin, and gray. The pattern appears zigzag-like, grayish, and shiny.

LEAF: It has simple, alternate, ovate-oblong leaves 2 to 5 inches long, with a tapering tip, and are coarsely serrated. The leaves are greenish-brown and glossy on the top and lighter green on the bottom.

FLOWER: American beech blooms with monoecious yellowish-green flowers from March to May. It forms large globular clusters of drooping, long-stemmed male flowers and short spikes of female flowers.

FRUIT/SEED/NUT: Two or three prickly husks remain on the tree after the nut has fallen, each approximately 3/4 inches long. September and October is the time when beechnuts ripen and become edible. The nuts drop to the ground in fall, typically around the first frost. If the beechnut shell has collapsed in on itself, or if there's a hole in the surface, it will likely be empty.

Look-a-likes: The European beechnut is edible but bitter. European beech trees resemble American beeches but have darker grey bark and shorter leaves.

Caution: none known

Culinary Preparation: As a herb, young leaves can be eaten raw or cooked. The leaves have a mild flavor but quickly become tough, so only use the youngest leaves. Despite their small size, the seeds have a lot of sweetness and nutrition. In addition to being rich in oil, they also contain up to 22% protein. You can make bread, cakes, or biscuits by drying and grinding them into a powder. Germinated seeds are safe to eat raw. They are crunchy, sweet, and nutty. Roasted seeds can be used as a substitute for coffee. The bark can be dried and ground into a powder and used as a thickener in soups or mixed with cereal when making bread.

Medicinal Uses: In treating frostbite, burns, poison ivy rash, and other skin conditions, boiled leaves have been used as a wash and poultice. Lung ailments have been treated with a tea made from the bark.

Fun or Historical Facts: Beechwood makes flooring, furniture, veneer plywood, and railroad ties. It is a favored wood for fuel because of its high density and good burning qualities. Coal tar made from beech wood protects the wood from rotting.

Dog Toxicity: Beechnuts are toxic for your pup. Dogs are prone to beech tree poisoning because they like the shape of the husk, where the most potent concentration of tannins is found. The size and weight of your dog will be a factor in the severity of the reaction and the quantity of beechnut they have eaten. Symptoms include nausea, vomiting, diarrhea, abdominal pain, fatigue, and dilated pupils.

B lack Walnut

juglans nigra [JOO-GLANZ NY-GRUH]

Black Walnuts are a delicacy, which means they're a fantastic find for foragers. They are native to the United States and belong to the Juglandaceae (walnut) family. They are delicious and relatively easy to forage, although you need to spend time processing them.

Locate: Black walnut trees grow in sunny areas, such as on the edges of forests, roadsides, or fields.

Identification:

GROWTH / SIZE: This native deciduous tree grows quickly and can reach heights of 75 feet.

BARK / STEM / ROOT: The stems range from black to brown and have V-shaped leaf scars with a bud inside. The mature bark is thick and brown. The rough diamond patterns on the bark are ridged and furrowed.

LEAF: In the spring, the leaves are 12 to 24 inches long, have 10 to 23 leaflets, ovate to lanceolate, and are finely serrated. It is common for leaves to fall sporadically during the season. In late spring, the leaves turn yellow-green; in the fall, they turn bright yellow.

FLOWER: During April and May, yellow-green, single-stemmed catkins appear in short spikes and are 2 1/2 to 5 1/2 inches long.

FRUIT/SEED/NUT: By October, the catkins become non-splitting, yellow-green husks that house an edible brown to black nut. These husks will begin to fall to the ground, which indicates they are ready for harvest. You can harvest earlier but must let the fruit ripen at home.

Look-a-like(s): Many native trees, such as sumac, walnut, and hickory, have similar leaf structures, but all are edible.

Caution: Black walnuts have a terrible habit of releasing a black juice that stains everything. Wear gloves and clothes you don't care about when harvesting and processing these nuts.

Culinary Preparation: If the nuts are still green, they will need a few days or weeks to ripen. Don't wash them; leave them to it. Once the hulls are soft to the touch, they're ripe. Wear old clothes and use a small mallet to crack the nuts, peel off the hulls and drop the walnuts into a big bucket of water. The walnuts are coated in black fluid and debris, so wash them thoroughly. Once they're clean, air dry, and don't let any critters nearby. Once completely dry, crack them with a heavy-duty nutcracker or nutpick and enjoy raw or roasted.

Medicinal Uses: As a supplement, black walnut is anti-parasitic and anti-fungal, helps increase digestive health, and helps to reduce excessive sweating.

Fun Fact: The early American settlers discovered black walnuts growing in mixed forests. The rich-brown heartwood is resistant to decay and is used in various building projects on the homestead where water or rain may be an issue, such as fence posts and windowsills. They also utilized the nuts from the trees as snacks while out in the fields, adding them to soups and stews or grinding them into a meal for baking. Because the nuts were so nutritious, they were collected and stored, unshelled, in the root cellars for the winter.

Dog Toxicity: The only acceptable answer is YES, but not for what you think. Walnut trees are susceptible to mold after a rainy spell, which is considered to cause toxicity in dogs. Symptoms of walnut poisoning are heavy panting, restlessness, excess salivation, vomiting, muscle tremors, fever, seizures, liver damage, and even death if left untreated.

White Oak

Quercus alba [KWER-kus AL-ba]

Almost everyone knows that whiskey is aged in charred new oak barrels, but did you know that barrels made of American white oak are also used for aging wine? It's part of the Fagaceae (walnut) family. It has several other names, Forked-leaf White Oak, Northern White Oak, and Quebec Oak, are just a few. The name is derived from the color of the finished wood.

Locate: It's usually found in forested areas of dry slopes, valleys, and ravines. You may find single trees in parks, fields, and meadows.

Identify:

GROWTH/SIZE - North America's eastern and central parts are home to this species. The oldest specimens have been documented to be over 450 years old. A mature tree typically reaches an elevation of 80–100 feet. The lower branches of this tree tend to extend far out laterally, parallel to the ground, leading to a massive canopy.

Bark/Stem - Smooth, light gray bark covers the branches. There are scattered white lenticels on the twigs, which are reddish-brown to purplish-brown. Generally, the bark is white or grayish and scaly. Furrows are shallow and divided into vertical blocks or flat, narrow plates. Over time, they will become flaky.

Leaf - Each leaf has five to nine deep, rounded, and even lobes and is 4 to 9 inches long and 2 to 4 inches wide. Their tip is rounded, and their base is wedge-shaped. Alternate, simple, elliptic, oblong, oblong-obovate, and cuneate leaves are found on this plant. Green in color, with a whitish or glaucous underside. It develops late in autumn and is purplish brown to reddish brown. A few leaves may persist into winter.

Flower - Blooming in April, the male flower is arranged in clusters of greenish-yellow catkins in long pendulous chains about 2 - 3 1/2 inches long. A female flower is not as showy and appears as a few greenish-red spots in the axils of emerging leaves.

Fruit/Nut - September through November is the time when the nuts appear. Initially green, they ripen to a light brown color. Fruits are 3/4 to 1-inch elongated acorns with shallow cups that cover 1/4 to 1/3 of the nut. Acorns mature in their first year and can be numerous.

Look-a-likes: none known

Caution: Look out for damaged acorns with holes or discoloration.

Prepare: First, put them in water and discard any floating to the top. Then, dry the acorns. Once they're dry, crack open the shells and grind or mash them. Finally, leach out the tannins in the acorns by soaking the mash in water. Leaching can take hours or weeks, and you may need to switch out the water periodically.

Medicinal Info/Use: In addition to its antiseptic and astringent properties, it is also an expectorant and tonic. Boiling the bark and drinking the liquid helps ease bleeding, diarrhea, fevers, coughs and colds, and asthma. Chewing the bark has helped to treat mouth ulcers. On the skin, it can be used as a wash to soothe burns, rashes, bruises, ulcers, etc., and on the vaginal area as a douche. Muscle pains have also been treated with it.

Fun Fact: The Japanese use white oak extensively for their martial arts weapons.

Pet Toxicity: Oak leaves and nuts contain gallic and tannic acids, which can harm pets. If eaten, symptoms are usually mild, including stomach discomfort, vomiting, and diarrhea.

Chanterelles
genus cantharellus [CAN-THA-REL-LUS]

Chanterelles come in many colors: Red, Golden, and Yellowfoot are just a few. Chanterelles are one of the ultimate wild mushrooms because they must be foraged rather than cultivated. Thankfully, they're easy to spot and delicious, with a peppery, earthy flavor.

Locate: Depending on its species; a chanterelle can be associated with conifers or hardwood trees. It is common to find them in forests with oaks, silver birches, Western hemlock trees, and Scots pine, especially when the undergrowth is moist and mossy. They are usually found in the same places as wild blueberries, but this is not guaranteed. A walk through the woods following rain should be fruitful from late July through September.

Identify:

CAP: This fruiting body is not separated into stalk and cap. It resembles a funnel with the opening expanded at the top. It can grow to a height of 4 inches and a diameter of 1/4-2 3/4 inches but has been reported to reach a maximum height of 6 inches on occasion.

FLESH: Aside from the Black trumpet we've discussed in a previous chapter, this genus has several species. They all have the same type of flesh but come in many colors ranging from whiteish yellow to orange.

SPORE: cream to buff

ODOR/TASTE: fragrant and fruity

Look-a-likes: The most common look-alike is the Jack-o-Lantern (*Omphalotus olearius*), which is the same color as the golden chanterelle. However, it has true gills. Chanterelles smell sweet and nutty when you pick them, but Jack-o-Lanterns don't.

Caution: none known

Prepare Clean well and store chanterelles in the refrigerator. Chanterelles work well in a lot of dishes or when fried in butter. You can also preserve them by drying them and turning them into a flavor-boosting powder. Generally, Chanterelles match well with eggs, curry, chicken, pork, fish, beef, and veal. They can be topped on pizzas, stewed, marinated, sautéed, or used as a filling for crêpes.

As you can see, Chanterelles can be added to many different dishes. It is common for mushroom enthusiasts to sauté chanterelles in butter with a pinch of salt, a clove of freshly crushed garlic, and a small amount of whipping cream. This recipe emphasizes the chanterelle flavor without being overpowered by other aromas. The recipe keeps its flavor after being frozen, which makes it an excellent option for lunches and dinners.

Medicinal Uses: Many species of chanterelles contain antioxidant carotenoids. Vitamin D is also abundant in them.

Chicken of the Woods

Laetiporus sulphureus [LAE-TI-POR-US SUL-PHU-REUS]

Chicken of the Woods is a striking, edible fungus that belongs to the Polyporaceae family. This shelf-like mushroom is known for its bright colors and unique texture that resembles the taste of chicken when cooked. Other common names for Chicken of the Woods include Sulphur Shelf and Crab-of-the-Woods.

Location: Chicken of the Woods is native to North America, including Texas, and is commonly found throughout the eastern, central, and southern parts of the state. It grows on hardwood trees, mainly oak, and occasionally on conifers. It is a saprotrophic mushroom, meaning it feeds on decaying wood, so it can often be found on dead or dying trees.

Identification:

CAP: The cap of is fan-shaped or semicircular, with a diameter ranging from 2 to 20 inches. The upper surface is smooth and brightly colored, usually in vivid yellow or orange shades.

Hymenium: The hymenium (the fertile, spore-producing surface) is composed of small, irregular pores on the underside of the cap. The pores are typically yellow or orange, becoming white or yellowish-white as the mushroom matures.

Stipe: It lacks a distinct stipe (stem) and is usually sessile, meaning it attaches directly to the wood without a supporting structure.

Spore Print: The spore print is white or pale yellowish.

Ecology: This mushroom is a saprotrophic decomposer, meaning it breaks down dead or decaying wood. It typically grows in overlapping clusters on the trunks or branches of hardwood trees and occasionally conifers.

Look-A-Like Plants: The **Jack O'Lantern mushroom** (*Omphalotus olearius*) can be mistaken for Chicken of the Woods due to its similar orange color, but it has a different structure with true gills and a distinct stem. Jack O'Lantern mushrooms are toxic and should not be consumed.

Cautions: While it is generally considered safe, some individuals may experience an allergic reaction or gastrointestinal upset after consumption. It is essential to cook it thoroughly and try a small amount first to avoid an adverse reaction. Avoid eating mushrooms growing on conifers or eucalyptus trees, as they may absorb toxic compounds from the wood.

Culinary Preparations: It's a popular edible mushroom due to its tender, chicken-like texture, and mild flavor. It can be sautéed, roasted, or used in soups, stews, and stir-fries. The mushroom's younger, more tender parts are the best for cooking.

Medicinal Uses: Traditionally, it has been used to boost the immune system and as an antimicrobial and anti-inflammatory agent. Modern research is limited, but some studies suggest it may have potential cancer-fighting properties due to the presence of specific polysaccharides.

Fun or Historical Fact: Chicken of the Woods has been a food source for centuries. Native Americans were known to use this mushroom for both culinary and medicinal purposes. In modern times, it has gained popularity among foragers and chefs for its unique texture and taste, earning it a spot on many gourmet menus.

King Bolete

boletus edulis [Bo-le-tus ed-u-lis]

Porcini mushrooms are members of the Boletaceae family. These highly sought-after fungi are renowned for their rich, earthy taste and meaty texture. Porcini mushrooms are also called King Bolete, Cep, Steinpilz, or Penny Bun. They have been used for culinary purposes for centuries, especially in Italian, French, and German cuisines.

Location: Porcini mushrooms are not native to Texas. They are native to the Northern Hemisphere, especially in Europe, North America, and Asia. They grow predominantly in coniferous and deciduous forests, usually in a symbiotic relationship with the roots of trees like pines, spruces, and firs.

Identification:

Cap: Porcini mushrooms have a large, rounded to, convex cap ranging from 2 to 10 inches in diameter. The cap is initially convex but becomes flatter as the mushroom matures. Its color varies from pale to dark brown; the surface is usually smooth and slightly sticky.

HYMENIUM: The hymenium of porcini mushrooms consists of pores instead of gills. When young, these small, round pores are white, turning yellowish and eventually greenish-yellow as they age.

STIPE: The stipe is thick, club-shaped, and is 2 to 8 inches long. It is typically white with fine, brownish reticulations (net-like pattern) covering the upper part of the stipe.

SPORE PRINT: Porcini mushrooms produce a brown spore print. To obtain a spore print, place the mushroom cap on a white or black paper sheet and cover it with a container. Leave it undisturbed for several hours or overnight, and you will see the spores deposited on the paper.

ECOLOGY: Porcini mushrooms are mycorrhizal fungi, meaning they form a symbiotic relationship with the roots of certain trees, helping them absorb nutrients while receiving sugars in return. Depending on the climate and location, they typically grow from late summer to early fall.

Look-A-Like Plants: There are some similar-looking mushrooms, such as the **Barrow's bolete** (*Boletus barrowsii*) and **Pine bolete (***Boletus pinophilus***)**, which are both considered edible and delicious. However, it's essential to be cautious with look-alikes, as some bolete mushrooms can be toxic, like the **Huron bolete (***Boletus huronensis).*

Cautions: As with any wild mushroom, it is crucial to be sure of your identification before consuming porcini mushrooms. Some toxic look-alikes can cause gastrointestinal distress, so always consult an expert or a reliable guidebook when in doubt.

Culinary Preparations: Porcini mushrooms are highly regarded in the culinary world and prized for their delicious, earthy flavor. They can be eaten fresh, sautéed, grilled, or added to soups, stews, and risottos. Porcini mushrooms can also be dried, intensifying their flavor and rehydrating them for various dishes.

Medicinal Uses: While porcini mushrooms are not widely recognized for their medicinal properties, they are rich in vitamins and minerals, such as potassium, copper, and selenium, and contain B vitamins and antioxidants. They can contribute to a healthy diet and provide essential nutrients.

Fun or Historical Fact: In Italy, porcini mushrooms are so highly valued that they have been given a "Denomination of Controlled Origin" (DOC) status in some regions, meaning that only mushrooms grown in specific areas can be labeled and sold as "Porcini." This is to maintain the quality and authenticity of these much-loved fungi.

L obster

hypomyces lactifluorum [HY-PO-MY-CES LAC-TI-FLOR-UM]

Lobster mushrooms are named such because they taste and smell like seafood, specifically lobsters. They're easy to identify because they look so bizarre. They are parasitic fungi, attacking other fungi and changing them drastically.

Locate: A lobster mushroom usually appears in deciduous woods with oaks and poplars in midsummer to early fall. They are often found near small ponds, clearings, and campsites in the forest.

Identify: Despite its common name, this is not a mushroom. Instead, it is a parasitic fungus that grows on mushrooms, making it a reddish-orange color similar to a lobster's shell. Lactarius, Lactifluus (milk caps), and Russula (brittle gills) are specifically affected.

FLESH: A hard, orange covering that attacks rapidly and quickly engulfs the host. The surface is dotted with tiny pimples.

Odor/Taste: They have a seafood-like flavor and a firm, dense texture.

Look-a-likes: As with any mushroom, approach cautiously and eat a small portion first.

Caution: Discard any with white mold.

Prepare: Clean any dirt and cook lightly with delicate flavors. Overcooking can interfere with the unique seafood flavor and texture. In excess, dried lobsters can become bitter. However, lobster mushrooms love contact with heat and fat. It is possible to curb any bitterness and deepen their flavor by exposing them to heat and fat, whether fresh or dried. A saffron/turmeric effect occurs when lobster mushrooms are exposed to fat and heat. A delicious risotto can be made with this, or compound butter can be made with this. Mix lobster mushrooms with other mushrooms to add a touch of variety to your cooking.

Medicinal Uses: Though considered healthy, lobster is not well-known as a medicinal mushroom.

Oyster

Pleurotus ostreatus [PLU-RO-TUS OS-TRE-TUS]

Oyster mushrooms are popular edible fungi known for their delicate texture and subtle flavor. They belong to the Pleurotaceae family and are not plants but rather a type of fungus. Other common names include Tree Oyster and Pearl Oyster Mushroom. Oyster mushrooms have been consumed for centuries for their culinary qualities and purported medicinal benefits.

Location: They are native to many parts of the world, including North America, Europe, and Asia. They can be found throughout Texas, growing on dead or dying hardwood trees, particularly beech, oak, and aspen.

Identification:

CAP: The cap typically ranges from 2 to 8 inches in diameter. It is fan-shaped or oyster-shaped and can be white, gray, or brown. The cap's surface is smooth and often slightly moist.

Hymenium: They have gills on the underside of the cap that run down the stem's base (if present). These gills are closely spaced, white to cream in color, and usually extend to the stem.

Stipe: They may have a short, stubby stem or none. When present, the stem is usually off-center and measures around 0.5 to 2 inches long.

Spore Print: The spore print is white to pale lilac-gray. To take a spore print, place the cap gill-side-down on a sheet of paper, cover it with a glass, and let it sit for several hours.

Ecology: They are saprotrophic fungi, meaning they decompose dead organic matter, helping recycle nutrients back into the ecosystem.

Look-A-Like Mushroom(s): One toxic look-alike is the **Angel's Wings** (*Pleurocybella porrigens),* smaller and thinner than the Oyster mushroom. Another potentially poisonous look-alike is the **Ivory Funnel** (*Clitocybe dealbata*), which has a more central stem and lacks the Oyster mushroom's distinctive gill pattern.

Cautions: Always exercise caution when foraging for mushrooms. Misidentification can lead to the ingestion of toxic species. Additionally, some people may experience allergic reactions or gastrointestinal upset after consuming Oyster mushrooms. If you're new to foraging, consult an experienced forager or a field guide to ensure proper identification.

Culinary Preparations: Oyster mushrooms are versatile and can be sautéed, roasted, or added to soups and stews—their delicate flavor pairs well with garlic, onions, and herbs. Be sure to clean and cook them thoroughly before eating, as raw Oyster mushrooms can be tough and slightly bitter.

Medicinal Uses: Traditionally, Oyster mushrooms have been used for their immune-boosting and cholesterol-lowering properties. Modern research suggests they contain compounds that may support heart health and have potential anticancer and antiviral effects.

A Fun Fact: Oyster mushrooms are delicious and environmentally friendly! They can be grown on agricultural waste products like straw, coffee grounds, and sawdust, making them a sustainable food source. Some innovative companies use Oyster mushrooms to break down and recycle hard-to-decompose materials like plastic and petroleum products.

W hite Morel

morchella americana [MOR-KEL-LA AMERICANA]

Morels are widely considered one of the best wild mushrooms that foragers can find. They are a native North American member of the **Morchellaceae** family. They're delicious and elusive enough that a fortunate forager typically keeps their morel spot close to their hearts.

Locate: Fruiting season is in spring for this species, mainly from March to June. They live in forests near more mature trees. Look around ash, elm, poplar, aspen, cottonwood, and apple trees for the best chance of finding them. Orchards are an excellent option. After forest fires, they thrive in logging areas, near streams, and loamy soil.

Identify:

CAP: Morchella americana has an egg-shaped head with a convex, bluntly conical, or almost round apex. There are pits and ridges in the head that are irregularly shaped, with broadly angled pits arranged either randomly or vertically. There is a yellow-to-brown coloration to the cap overall. It is worth noting that the depth and color of the cap's ridges and pits differ depending on the age of the mushroom. The cap is attached directly to the stalk without a significant overhang or rim. The average height of the cap is between 1/2 - 2 inches, but it can grow as tall as 4 inches. The cap measures approximately 1/2 to 2 inches wide.

STEM: The stem measures 1 to 4 inches tall and 1/2 to 4 inches wide. The stem is usually shorter than the cap. The stem is finely granular in texture and swollen at the base. The stem is hollow, but sometimes it can be chambered near the bottom. The stem is a pale yellow to tan.

FLESH: it is whitish to pale yellowish or brownish

Look-a-likes: Fortunately, eating most true morels is safe, so the mix-up shouldn't be a severe issue.

Caution: False morels might have wrinkly caps, but they look more like brains than honeycombs. Inspect the mushroom thoroughly before you harvest it, as insects have hollowed out some toxic false morels.

Harvest: Morels grow in the spring, usually between March and late May or early June.

Prepare: Morels are tricky to clean, so you may need to soak them to eliminate dirt, bugs, or other debris. It would be best if you cooked morels, and a great way to get the most out of them is to sauté them in butter.

Medicinal Uses: The use of morels as a medicinal plant dates back centuries. They have been known for their health-related benefits. They have been studied for bioactive properties, including anti-oxidative and anti-inflammatory properties and immunostimulatory and anti-tumor effects.

PART FOUR

THE LUSCIOUS BOUNTY OF TEXAS

FRUITS AND BERRIES OF THE LONE STAR STATE

A garita

Mahonia trifoliolata [MA-HO-NEE-UH TRY-FOH-LEE-OH-LAY-TUH]

Agarita is a member of the Berberidaceae family and a plant with a plethora of names. Some may know it as the Texas Wild Currant or Berberis trifoliolata, while others call it Chaparral Berry. Regardless of its moniker, Agarita has been stealing the show for centuries. Initially, the Native Americans were quite fond of Agarita, as it served multiple purposes. They cleverly used the bright red berries for food and dyes, while the roots were employed as a yellow dye and for medicinal purposes. Talk about a versatile plant, right?

Location: Agarita is a bit particular about where it grows. This prickly superstar is in Texas, New Mexico, and Arizona. It thrives in dry, rocky environments and can often be found hanging out with the junipers and oaks in woodlands and chaparral.

Identification:

GROWTH/SIZE: Agarita is a modest shrub, typically growing between 36-72 inches tall and wide.

Bark/Stem/Root: Its bark is thin and grayish, while the stems are a bit more flashy, adorned with rigid, sharp, trifoliate leaves.

Leaf: Each leaf measures about 3/4-1 inch long and is divided into three leaflets with spiny, serrated edges.

Flower: Agarita boasts fragrant, golden-yellow flowers in late winter or early spring that measure about 1/2 inch across.

Fruit/Seed/Nut: The fruits, or berries, are bright red, spherical, and around 1/4-1/2 inch in diameter.

Look-A-Like Plants: Agarita has a few look-a-likes, including the non-toxic **Oregon Grape** (*Mahonia aquifolium*) and the toxic **Holly** (*Ilex spp.*). But worry not; Agarita's trifoliate leaves and penchant for drier climates help set it apart from its doppelgängers.

Culinary preparations: the tart red berries can be turned into jellies, jams, or even wine.

Medicinal uses: the roots were known to treat ailments like fever and stomach disorders. Modern research has shown that the plant contains berberine, which has antimicrobial and anti-inflammatory properties.

Fun or Historical Fact: During the Texas Revolution, Agarita was used as a source of vitamin C to prevent scurvy among soldiers. Talk about an under-appreciated hero!

Dog toxicity: Agarita berries are not known to be toxic to our furry friends. Signs of plant ingestion may include vomiting, diarrhea, or other unusual behavior.

American Beautyberry

Callicarpa americana [KUH-LIK-AR-PUH UH-MER-IH-KAN-UH]

Let's dive into the vibrant world of the American Beautyberry! This stunning plant belongs to the Verbenaceae family. Other common names include French mulberry and sourbush. Native Americans initially used the American Beautyberry for various purposes, from medicinal remedies to insect repellents.

Location: It's native to the southeastern United States, including the eastern and central parts of Texas. This lovely plant can be found in woodlands, forest edges, and along stream banks, where it enjoys the dappled shade and moist, well-drained soils.

Identification:

GROWTH/SIZE: A deciduous shrub typically grows between 3 and 6 feet tall, although it can sometimes reach up to 9 feet.

Bark/Stem/Root: The bark is thin, with a smooth grayish-brown surface. The stems are slender, arching, and tend to grow in clumps, while the root system is fibrous and shallow.

Leaf: The leaves are simple, opposite, and ovate to elliptical. They measure 4 to 8 inches long and 2 to 4 inches wide, with serrated margins. The leaves are bright green on top and paler green underneath.

Flower: It produces small, pink, or lavender flowers that bloom from June to August. The flowers are clustered in groups, appearing along the stems at leaf axils.

Fruit/Seed/Nut: The plant's most striking feature is its clusters of vibrant magenta berries that encircle the stems. Each berry is approximately 1/4 inch in diameter and contains a few small seeds.

Look-A-Like Plants: American Beautyberry could be mistaken for the non-native and invasive **Chinese Beautyberry** (*Callicarpa dichotoma*). However, the native American Beautyberry has larger leaves and fruits than the Chinese variety, which has a more compact growth habit.

Cautions: None known.

Culinary Preparations: The berries can be eaten raw but are somewhat astringent. They are often used to make jelly, syrup, or wine, providing a unique and delightful flavor.

Medicinal Uses: Historically, Native Americans used leaves and roots to treat various ailments, such as fever, dysentery, and colic. The crushed leaves were also applied as a natural insect repellent. Modern research on the plant's medicinal properties is limited, so it's best to consult a professional before using it medicinally.

Fun or Historical Fact: It's a favorite among many bird species, which feast on the bright berries during the fall and winter. This helps to spread the seeds and ensure the plant's continued propagation throughout its native range.

Dog Toxicity: There is no evidence to suggest that American Beautyberry is toxic to dogs. If your dog shows symptoms like vomiting, diarrhea, or loss of appetite after ingesting parts of the plant, consult your veterinarian for advice.

F arkleberry

Vaccinium arboreum [VUH-SIN-ee-um ar-BORE-ee-um]

Farkleberry is a fascinating shrub belonging to the Ericaceae family. It's also known as the Tree Huckleberry, Sparkleberry, or Farklebush. Now, doesn't that roll off the tongue? This alluring berry has been a star in the botanical world for centuries. Native Americans had a sweet spot for Farkleberries, using the fruits as a source of nourishment and occasionally employing the plant's parts for medicinal purposes.

Location: It grows in a variety of habitats across the southeastern United States. You can find these shrubs in sandy, well-drained soils, and they're often spotted in the company of oaks and pines in open woods, hammocks, and swamps.

Identification:

GROWTH/SIZE: Farkleberry is quite the showstopper, reaching heights between 3 and 15 feet tall, depending on its environment.

Bark/Stem/Root: The bark is thin and reddish-brown, adding a splash of color to the landscape. Its stems and roots are slender and wiry, giving it a unique, whimsical appearance.

Leaf: Each simple, elliptical leaf measures 1-3 inches long, featuring a leathery texture and a lustrous, dark green hue.

Flower: It loves to put on a show with its small, white, bell-shaped flowers that measure around 1/4 inch long. These flowers are ready to party in late spring or early summer.

Fruit/Seed/Nut: The fruits are small, dark blue to black berries, measuring approximately 1/4-1/2 inch in diameter. They're quite the eye-catching treat!

Look-A-Like Plants: Farkleberry has a few look-a-likes, including the non-toxic **Highbush Blueberry** (*Vaccinium corymbosum*) and the toxic **Buckthorn** (*Rhamnus* spp.). Farkleberry's unique, leathery leaves and preference for particular habitats help it stand out from the crowd.

Cautions: While Farkleberry is generally considered safe, it's always best to exercise caution when foraging for wild plants.

Culinary Preparations: Farkleberries can be used in various culinary creations, including jams, jellies, and pies. Some even claim the berries make a fabulous wine, adding a touch of sparkle to any occasion.

Medicinal Uses: Traditionally, Native Americans used Farkleberry to treat various ailments, such as digestive issues and fever. In comparison, modern medicine has not extensively studied Farkleberry's medicinal properties.

Fun or Historical Fact: Did you know that Farkleberry is a deciduous plant that sheds its leaves annually? This adds a touch of fiery color to the fall landscape, making Farkleberry a true seasonal sensation.

Dog Toxicity: Good news for our canine companions: Farkleberries are not known to be toxic to dogs. Symptoms of plant ingestion may include vomiting, diarrhea, or other unusual behavior.

F lameleaf Sumac

Rhus lanceolata [ROOS LAN-SEE-OH-LAH-TUH]

Flameleaf Sumac is a striking member of the Anacardiaceae family. This show-stopping plant, also known as Prairie Flameleaf Sumac or Texas Sumac, has been valued for its ornamental appeal and usefulness in traditional medicine and as a source of dye.

Location: A true Texan, Flameleaf Sumac is native to the Lone Star State, particularly in the central, northern, and western regions. This hardy plant thrives in a range of habitats, from rocky slopes and limestone outcrops to open woodlands and grasslands. It's a proud Texan standing tall in the face of adversity and making the landscape a little more vibrant.

Identification:

GROWTH / SIZE: A small, deciduous tree or large shrub that typically reaches heights of 6-15 feet. Its size and form make it a splendid choice for adding visual interest to your landscape.

Bark/Stem/Root: The bark is rough and dark gray, contrasting the bright foliage. Stems are slender and reddish-brown, while the roots are sturdy and deep, anchoring the plant securely.

Leaf: The show's star, Flameleaf Sumac's compound leaves measure 6-12 inches long and comprise numerous lance-shaped leaflets. The leaves boast a brilliant green hue in spring and summer, turning to a fiery red in the fall, setting the landscape ablaze with color.

Flower: the flowers are small, greenish-white, and arranged in dense, cone-shaped clusters measuring about 3-5 inches long. They bloom from late spring to early summer, attracting bees and butterflies to the garden.

Fruit/Seed/Nut: Following the flowers, Flameleaf Sumac produces clusters of small, round, red fruit, each measuring about 1/16 inch in diameter. These fruits, known as drupes, persist into the winter and provide a food source for birds and other wildlife.

Look-A-Like Plants: It can be confused with other sumac species, such as **Staghorn Sumac** (*Rhus typhina*) or **Smooth Sumac** (*Rhus glabra*). Fortunately, all these sumac species are non-toxic and share similar properties, making identification errors less of a concern.

Cautions: While Flameleaf Sumac is generally considered safe, some individuals may experience skin irritation or allergic reactions when handling the plant, especially if they are sensitive to other members of the Anacardiaceae family, like poison ivy.

Culinary Preparations: Flameleaf Sumac's tart, red drupes can be used to make a refreshing, lemonade-like drink called "sumac-ade." Simply soak the drupes in cold water, strain, and sweeten to taste. The fruit can also be dried and ground into a tangy, crimson spice that adds a burst of flavor to various dishes.

Medicinal Uses: Traditionally, Flameleaf Sumac has been used by Native American tribes to treat a variety of ailments, including fever, digestive issues, and skin conditions. The leaves, bark, and roots were also used to make a range of medicinal teas and poultices.

Fun or Historical Fact: Flameleaf Sumac's vibrant fall foliage made it a popular choice for use in ornamental landscaping, particularly in the 19th and 20th centuries. It was—and still is—admired for its ability to create a stunning visual impact with its fiery autumn hues.

Dog Toxicity: Good news for dog lovers: Flameleaf Sumac is not toxic to dogs. However, it's still important to keep an eye on your furry friends when they're around plants.

I ndian Fig

Opuntia ficus-indica [OH-PUN-TEE-UH FIK-US IN-DIH-KUH]

This intriguing plant belongs to the Cactaceae family and goes by a few other common names, such as Nopal, Sabra, or Tuna. Its original use? Well, this versatile plant has been used for food, medicine, and even building materials by indigenous peoples for centuries.

Location: It's native to the arid regions of the Americas, including the southwestern United States, Mexico, and South America. In Texas, it's found in various areas, from deserts to grasslands, and is especially abundant in the western and southern parts of the state.

Identification:

GROWTH/SIZE: It exhibits a wide range of sizes, with some species reaching up to 16 feet tall! However, most species typically grow between 2 to 6 feet in height.

Bark/Stem/Root: The plant's stems are large, fleshy, and flat, known as "pads" or "nopales," and can be 4 to 18 inches long and 3 to 12 inches wide. The roots are fibrous and spread horizontally, helping the plant absorb water in its dry native environment.

Leaf: Technically, Prickly Pear Cactus doesn't have leaves. Instead, it has modified stems that photosynthesize and store water.

Flower: The flowers are vibrant and showy, usually in shades of yellow, red, or orange. They measure 2 to 3 inches in diameter and bloom between April and June.

Fruit/Seed/Nut: The fruit, called "tunas," are oval-shaped, typically 1 to 2 inches long, and can range in color from green to red or purple. They contain small, hard seeds.

Look-A-Like Plants: There aren't many look-a-like plants, as their unique appearance sets them apart. However, other cacti species, such as the **Cholla** (*Cylindropuntia spp.*), can sometimes be mistaken for Prickly Pear.

Cautions: Be cautious when handling; it's covered in spines and tiny hair-like barbs called "glochids" that can easily become lodged in the skin, causing irritation and discomfort.

Culinary Preparations: It has been used as a culinary ingredient for generations. The nopales can be prepared like vegetables, while the tunas can be eaten fresh, juiced, or made into jams and jellies.

Medicinal Uses: Traditionally, it's been used to treat a variety of ailments, including wounds, burns, and digestive issues. Modern research suggests that it may be beneficial for managing diabetes and high cholesterol levels.

Fun or Historical Fact: Prickly Pear Cactus played a crucial role in the Mexican coat of arms! Legend has it that the Aztecs were instructed by their god, Huitzilopochtli [WEE-TSEE-LOH-POCH-TLEE], to build their city where they found an eagle perched on a cactus, devouring a snake. The cactus in question? None other than the Prickly Pear!

Dog Toxicity: Prickly Pear Cactus is not toxic to dogs, but the spines and glochids can cause physical harm if ingested or lodged in their skin.

M ayhaw
Crataegus opaca [KRUH-TEE-GUS OH-PAK-UH]

Mayhaw is a small tree belonging to the Rosaceae family. It has other charming names like May Hawthorn or Apple Haw. This delightful tree has a long history of captivating hearts with its beautiful blooms and tantalizing fruits.

Location: Mayhaw is a native Texan, but it doesn't stop there. These lovely trees are scattered throughout the southeastern United States, from Florida to Louisiana. They grow in wet, swampy areas or along the banks of streams and rivers, providing picturesque scenery for those who are fortunate enough to stumble upon them.

Identification:

GROWTH/SIZE: Mayhaw trees are modest in size, generally reaching heights of 15-30 feet.

Bark/Stem/Root: Their bark is scaly and reddish-brown, while the stems and roots are slender and woody, just perfect for supporting the tree's delicate foliage and fruits.

Leaf: Each simple, elliptical leaf measures about 1-3 inches long, with serrated margins and a vibrant green hue that adds a touch of freshness to the landscape.

Flower: In spring, Mayhaw trees put on a dazzling display with white or pink flowers measuring around 1/2 inch in diameter. Talk about a sight for sore eyes!

Fruit/Seed/Nut: The fruits are small, round, and typically red, resembling miniature apples. They measure about 1/2-1 inch in diameter and are a real treat for those who can harvest them.

Look-A-Like Plants: Mayhaw shares some resemblance with other **Hawthorns** (*Crataegus* spp.), which are generally non-toxic. However, always make sure to identify the plant you're encountering correctly. A key feature distinguishing Mayhaw from its look-a-likes is the habitat where it grows: wet, swampy areas or near water sources.

Cautions: While Mayhaw is generally safe, it's always wise to be cautious when foraging for wild plants.

Culinary Preparations: Mayhaw fruits are the stars of the culinary world, especially in the South. They can be turned into delicious jellies, jams, and even wines, adding a burst of fruity flavor to any meal.

Medicinal Uses: Although Mayhaw has not been extensively studied for its medicinal properties, it's worth noting that other Hawthorns are traditionally used to treat cardiovascular conditions. Who knows? Perhaps Mayhaw shares some of these benefits, too.

Fun or Historical Fact: In parts of the southeastern United States, Mayhaw is celebrated with annual festivals dedicated to these delightful fruits. The events often include jelly-making contests and other fun-filled activities that showcase the local love for Mayhaw.

Dog Toxicity: Mayhaw fruits are not known to be toxic to dogs. Symptoms of plant ingestion may include vomiting, diarrhea, or other unusual behavior. If you suspect your dog has ingested an unknown plant, consult your veterinarian.

Mustang Grape

Vitis mustangensis [VI-tis mus-TAN-jen-sis]

Mustang Grape is a vivacious vine belonging to the Vitaceae family. Known by other endearing names such as the Texas Wild Grape or Wild Mustang Grape, this rugged vine has been a fan favorite for centuries, valued for its hardy nature and versatile fruit.

Location: As a true native of the Lone Star State, the Mustang Grape thrives in various regions of Texas, predominantly in the eastern, central, and southern parts. This wild grape is not one to shy away from a challenge, as it can be found in woodlands, along fences, and sprawled across the landscape, embracing Texas's wild, untamed spirit.

Identification:

Growth/Size: Mustang Grape vines can grow to an impressive 60 feet or more, climbing and entwining themselves around trees and other structures for support.

Bark/Stem/Root: The bark is brown and shreddy, while the stems are slender, woody, and equipped with forked tendrils that help the vine cling to its surroundings.

Leaf: Each leaf is a stunning work of art, measuring about 3-5 inches long and featuring a heart-shaped or lobed appearance. The upper surface is a glossy green, while the lower surface is coated with a layer of fuzzy, white hairs.

Flower: In the late spring, it bursts into bloom, showcasing its small, greenish-white flowers in clusters that measure around 2-4 inches long.

Fruit/Seed/Nut: The fruits are small, round grapes that measure approximately 1/2-1 inch in diameter. They're usually dark purple or black with thick, inedible skin and contain large seeds.

Look-A-Like Plants: Mustang Grape shares some resemblance with other grape species (*Vitis* spp.), which are generally non-toxic. The thick-skinned, tart grapes and fuzzy, white-haired leaves set Mustang Grape apart from other grapevines.

Cautions: Mustang Grape is generally safe for consumption.

Culinary Preparations: Mustang Grapes are a versatile ingredient in the kitchen, perfect for making jelly, juice, and even wine. While their skin is quite thick and sour, the pulp offers a unique, tart flavor that can add a zesty kick to your culinary creations.

Medicinal Uses: Mustang Grape has not been widely studied for its medicinal properties. However, it's worth noting that grapes, in general, are a rich source of antioxidants and other beneficial nutrients, which may offer various health benefits.

Fun or Historical Fact: The Mustang Grape has a long-standing history in Texas, with records dating back to the 16th century when Spanish explorers documented the vine's presence. Its wild, untamed nature embodies the spirit of the land where it thrives.

Dog Toxicity: Grapes, including Mustang Grapes, are toxic to dogs and can cause serious health issues. If your dog ingests any grapes, symptoms may include vomiting, diarrhea, lethargy, abdominal pain, and kidney failure.

S and Plum

Prunus angustifolia [PROO-NUS AN-GUS-TI-FOH-LEE-UH]

Sand Plum belongs to the Rosaceae family. This delightful little fruit goes by other names, such as Chickasaw Plum, Sandhill Plum, and Peach Bush. Sand Plums have been gracing the landscape with their beauty and flavor for generations, making them a beloved staple in many a pantry.

Location: Sand Plums are native to the southern United States, including Texas. You'll most likely find them in the central and eastern regions of the Lone Star State. These hardy plants are adaptable, thriving in sandy soil, open woodlands, and along roadsides and riverbanks.

Identification:

GROWTH/SIZE: A small, deciduous shrub or tree, typically reaching heights of 4-20 feet, spreading its branches in a lovely, rounded shape.

Bark/Stem/Root: The bark is dark and scaly, while the stems and roots are slender and woody, providing the perfect framework for the plant's lush foliage.

Leaf: Each leaf is slender and elongated, measuring about 1-3 inches long. The leaves boast a beautiful shade of green and are finely toothed along the margins.

Flower: Sand Plums put on a spectacular show in early spring with their delicate white flowers. Each bloom measures approximately 1/2 inch in diameter, creating a stunning contrast against the plant's green foliage.

Fruit/Seed/Nut: The fruits are small, round plums that measure about 1/2-1 inch in diameter. They can vary in color from yellow to deep red and have a delightfully sweet taste that's hard to resist.

Look-A-Like Plants: Sand Plums bear a resemblance to other plum species (*Prunus* spp.), which are generally non-toxic. The slender leaves and small, round fruits are distinctive features of Sand Plums that can help differentiate them from other species.

Cautions: None known.

Culinary Preparations: Sand Plums are a scrumptious treat that can be enjoyed fresh or used in various culinary creations. Their sweet, tangy flavor makes them perfect for jams, jellies, pies, and even homemade wines. Your taste buds will thank you for including these delightful fruits in your recipes!

Medicinal Uses: Although not extensively studied for their medicinal properties, plums, in general, are known to be rich in vitamins, minerals, and antioxidants. These nutrients can offer various health benefits, so don't be surprised if Sand Plums have some hidden gems of their own.

Fun or Historical Fact: The Chickasaw people, native to the southeastern United States, traditionally used Sand Plum branches to construct a type of traditional dwelling called a "winter house." The plant's versatility and importance to the Chickasaw people demonstrate the fascinating connection between humans and the natural world.

Dog Toxicity: Sand Plums are not known to be toxic to dogs.

S oapberry

Sapindus saponaria [SUH-PIN-DUS SUH-PUH-NAIR-EE-UH]

Let's lather up with some fascinating history about Soap Berries! These frothy fruits belong to the Sapindaceae family and are also known as Soap Nuts, Soapberry Trees, or Western Soapberry. Their original use? You guessed it - as a natural soap, thanks to the presence of saponins in the fruit.

Location: Soap Berries are native to the southern and central regions of the United States, including Texas. They are often found in limestone soils along streams, canyons, and wooded hillsides.

Identification:

GROWTH/SIZE: Soap Berries can grow into small to medium-sized trees, usually reaching heights between 10 and 50 feet.

BARK/STEM/ROOT: The bark of Soap Berries is gray to reddish-brown and becomes furrowed and scaly with age. Its stems and branches are slender and often have a slight zigzag pattern.

Leaf: Soap Berry leaves are pinnately compound, measuring 4 to 12 inches long, with 6 to 18 leaflets. Each leaflet is 1 to 2 inches long and has a lanceolate shape with a pointed tip.

Flower: The flowers of Soap Berries are small, greenish-white, and fragrant. They appear in clusters, measuring around 3 to 8 inches long, and bloom from May to July.

Fruit/Seed/Nut: Soap Berries produce small, round, and translucent yellow fruits about 1/2 inch in diameter. The fruits contain a large, black, and shiny seed.

Look-A-Like Plants: The Chinaberry tree (Melia azedarach) has similar leaves and fruit, but it's toxic and should not be confused with the Soap Berry.

Cautions: Although the fruit of the Soap Berry is not toxic, ingesting large quantities may cause gastrointestinal distress. Also, be cautious when using the fruit as soap, as some individuals may have allergic reactions to the saponins.

Culinary Preparations: Soap Berries are not typically used for culinary purposes, primarily for their soap-making properties.

Medicinal Uses: In traditional medicine, the bark, roots, and leaves of the Soap Berry tree have been used to treat various ailments such as skin conditions, digestive issues, and fevers. However, more research is needed to confirm the effectiveness of these uses.

Fun or Historical Fact: Soap Berries have been used by Native Americans and pioneers alike as a natural soap alternative. The fruit can be crushed and mixed with water to create a lathering solution perfect for cleaning clothes, hair, or even dishes!

Dog Toxicity: Soap Berries are not considered toxic to dogs, but ingesting large quantities may cause gastrointestinal upset. Consult your veterinarian for symptoms such as vomiting, diarrhea, or lethargy.

Spanish Daggerfruit

Yucca treculeana [YUH-KUH TREH-KOO-LEE-AY-NUH]

This spiky plant belongs to the Asparagaceae family and is known as Yucca treculeana, Spanish Bayonet, or Don Quixote's Lance. Native Americans and early settlers found a variety of purposes for this versatile plant, including using its fibers for making rope, clothing, and baskets, as well as consuming its flowers and fruit.

Location: It's native to Texas, specifically the south and central regions. It thrives in a variety of habitats, from coastal dunes to rocky hillsides and limestone slopes.

Identification:

GROWTH/SIZE: It can grow up to 10 to 15 feet tall, with a trunk diameter of about 8 inches. The plant has a tree-like growth habit with a single or branched trunk.

Bark/Stem/Root: The bark is grayish-brown and rough. Its stems are rigid and fibrous, while the roots are shallow and extensive, allowing the plant to absorb water quickly.

Leaf: The leaves are long, rigid, and sword-shaped, measuring 20 to 40 inches long and 1 to 2 inches wide. They are blue-green to grayish-green, with sharp, pointy tips and serrated edges.

Flower: The flowers are white or cream-colored, bell-shaped, and fragrant. They grow in dense, erect clusters at the top of a tall stalk, reaching up to 3 feet, and typically bloom from April to June.

Fruit/Seed/Nut: It produces a fleshy, green fruit that matures to a dark brown or black color. The fruit measures 2 to 3 inches long and contains numerous small, flat, black seeds.

Look-A-Like Plants: It can be easily confused with other yucca species, such as **Spanish Bayonet** (*Yucca gloriosa*) and **Aloe Yucca** (*Yucca aloifolia*). However, these plants are not toxic and can be differentiated by examining their leaves, flowers, and habitat preferences.

Cautions: Exercise caution when handling Spanish Dagger, as its leaves have sharp points and serrated edges that can cause injury. Additionally, some people may experience skin irritation from contact with the plant's sap.

Culinary Preparations: The flowers and fruit are edible and can be consumed raw or cooked. Flowers are often used in salads, while the fruit can be baked or roasted. Always correctly identify the plant and remove any sharp or fibrous parts before consuming.

Medicinal Uses: Traditionally, Native Americans used Spanish Daggerfruit for its anti-inflammatory and pain-relieving properties. They applied crushed roots and leaves to wounds, sores, and aching joints. However, modern research is limited, and further studies are needed to confirm these medicinal uses.

Fun or Historical Fact: It has been used historically as a source of soap. The roots and trunk contain saponins, which can be extracted and used as a natural soap or shampoo when mixed with water.

Dog Toxicity: Spanish Dagger is not known to be toxic to dogs. However, the sharp leaves can cause physical injuries to dogs if they come into contact with the plant. If your dog experiences symptoms like pain, swelling, or skin irritation after contact with the plant, consult your veterinarian for advice.

S weet Acacia

Vachellia farnesiana [VUH-KEL-ee-uh FAR-NUH-SEE-uh-NUH]

Sweet Acacia is a mesmerizing plant belonging to the Fabaceae family. This alluring tree is also known by other names such as Huisache, Cassie, or Needle Bush. Sweet Acacia has been admired for centuries, praised for its breathtaking beauty, delightful fragrance, and many practical uses.

Location: Sweet Acacia is a true Texan native, found predominantly in the southern and central regions of the Lone Star State. This enchanting tree adores the sun's warm embrace and prefers well-drained soil. You can spot Sweet Acacia brightening up landscapes in open woodlands, along roadsides, or even gracing urban settings with its presence.

Identification:

GROWTH/SIZE: A small to medium-sized tree, usually reaching heights of 15-30 feet. Its rounded, spreading crown makes it a striking addition to any landscape.

BARK/STEM/ROOT: The bark is grayish-brown with shallow fissures, while the stems are armed with sharp, slender thorns that can reach up to 2 inches long.

LEAF: Each delicate, feathery leaf is composed of numerous tiny, oval leaflets measuring only around 1/4 inch long. The leaves have a graceful, fern-like appearance that adds to the tree's allure.

FLOWER: Sweet Acacia's true claim to fame lies in its stunning, fragrant flowers. These small, golden-yellow puffballs measure about 1/2 inch in diameter and release an enchanting, sweet aroma that is simply irresistible.

FRUIT/SEED/NUT: The fruits are elongated, flat, and brown seed pods measuring about 1-3 inches long. Each pod contains several small, hard seeds.

Look-A-Like Plants: Sweet Acacia can be easily confused with other species of Acacia or even **Mesquite** (*Prosopis spp.*). However, Sweet Acacia's fragrant, golden-yellow flowers and slender, sharp thorns help distinguish it from these look-alikes, which are generally non-toxic.

Cautions: While Sweet Acacia is not considered toxic, the tree's sharp thorns can pose a risk of injury. Always exercise caution when approaching or handling the tree to avoid unpleasant encounters.

Culinary Preparations: Sweet Acacia flowers are the star of the show in culinary preparations. Their delightful fragrance can infuse sugars and syrups or even create exquisite floral jelly. Let your creativity soar as you explore this enchanting tree's myriad possibilities!

Medicinal Uses: Traditionally, Sweet Acacia has been used for various medicinal purposes, including treating skin conditions and respiratory issues, and as an antispasmodic. Modern research is limited; however, some studies suggest that Sweet Acacia extracts may possess antimicrobial and antioxidant properties.

Fun or Historical Fact: Sweet Acacia flowers have been used for centuries in the French perfume industry, lending their enchanting fragrance to some of the world's most iconic scents. The tree's timeless allure truly transcends borders and generations.

Dog Toxicity: Sweet Acacia is not known to be toxic to dogs. However, the tree's sharp thorns can cause injury to curious pets. It's always best to keep an eye on your furry friend outdoors and consult a veterinarian if you suspect any injuries or ingestion of an unknown plant.

Texas Persimmon

Diospyros texana [DYE-OSS-PIH-ROSS TEHKS-AH-NUH]

Texas Persimmon is a delectable fruit that belongs to the Ebenaceae family. This charming plant is also known as Black Persimmon, Chapote, and Mexican Persimmon, among other captivating monikers. Texas Persimmon has been cherished for its sweet, dark fruits and sturdy, attractive wood for generations.

Location: Texas Persimmon is native to, you guessed it, Texas! You'll find it mainly in the central, southern, and western regions of the Lone Star State. This resilient plant is versatile, thriving in rocky hillsides, limestone slopes, and riverbanks. Keep your eyes peeled, and you might spot one of these beauties in its natural habitat!

Identification:

GROWTH/SIZE: A small, deciduous tree or large shrub, typically reaching heights of 15-40 feet. Its multi-trunked structure adds an artistic flair to the landscape.

BARK/STEM/ROOT: The bark is smooth and gray, often peeling away to reveal a striking white or cream-colored layer beneath. The tree's stems and roots are strong and woody, providing a sturdy foundation for its lush foliage.

LEAF: Each simple, elliptical leaf measures about 1-3 inches long, boasting a lovely shade of green that contrasts beautifully with the tree's striking bark.

FLOWER: During spring, Texas Persimmon sports small, inconspicuous flowers. The blooms are white to greenish-yellow and measure approximately 1/4-1/2 inches in diameter.

FRUIT/SEED/NUT: The real treasure lies in its fruits—small, round persimmons that measure about 3/4-1 1/2 inches in diameter. These sweet, black fruits are a tasty treat for humans and wildlife.

Look-A-Like Plants: Texas Persimmon can be easily confused with other species, such as the **American Persimmon** (*Diospyros virginiana*). However, Texas Persimmon's smooth, peeling bark and smaller fruits help distinguish it from its look-alikes, which are generally non-toxic.

Cautions: None known.

Culinary Preparations: Texas Persimmons are a scrumptious treat that can be enjoyed fresh or used in a variety of culinary creations. Their sweet flavor makes them perfect for jams, jellies, pies, and even smoothies. Get ready to indulge your taste buds with these delightful fruits!

Medicinal Uses: While not extensively studied for its medicinal properties, Texas Persimmon has been traditionally used to treat digestive issues, particularly diarrhea. The fruit's astringent properties were believed to help alleviate these symptoms.

Fun or Historical Fact: Native American tribes, such as the Comanche, have been known to use Texas Persimmon wood to create tools, including digging sticks and bows, highlighting the plant's versatility and importance in their culture.

Dog Toxicity: Texas Persimmons are not known to be toxic to dogs.

Yellow Passionfruit

Passiflora lutea [PUH-SIF-LOR-UH LOO-TEE-UH]

Yellow Passionfruit is a vibrant and alluring member of the Passifloraceae family. This luscious tropical fruit has charmed taste buds for centuries and goes by other whimsical names such as Golden Passionfruit or Sweet Granadilla. It was initially cultivated for its juicy, tangy fruit, which has become a beloved ingredient in many culinary creations.

Location: While Yellow Passionfruit is not native to Texas, it can grow in warmer climates or greenhouses. It originates from South America, basking in the tropical sun, spreading its tendrils and vivacious flowers across trellises and fences. If you're keen on cultivating this exotic beauty in Texas, you'll need to provide it with a warm, sheltered spot with ample sunlight.

Identification:

GROWTH/SIZE: A vigorous climbing vine that can reach lengths of up to 50 feet or more. It's known for its rapid growth, especially in warm, sunny conditions.

BARK/STEM/ROOT: The slender, woody stems are adorned with tendrils that help the plant climb and twine around supporting structures. The roots are robust and deep, enabling the plant to access nutrients and moisture.

LEAF: Each glossy, green, three-lobed leaf measures approximately 3-8 inches long. The leaves provide a lush, tropical backdrop for the plant's vibrant flowers and fruits.

FLOWER: The flowers are a true spectacle, with intricate, showy blooms about 2-3 inches across. The flowers boast a unique structure, featuring a central corona of white and purple filaments surrounded by delicate, fringed petals.

FRUIT/SEED/NUT: The fruit is a round or oval, yellow-skinned capsule measuring 2-3 inches in diameter. The interior is filled with an aromatic, juicy pulp dotted with numerous small, black seeds.

Look-A-Like Plants: Yellow Passionfruit could be mistaken for other passionfruit species (*Passiflora* spp.), such as the **Purple Passionfruit** (*Passiflora ligularis*), which is also non-toxic. The primary distinguishing feature is the color of the fruit, with Yellow Passionfruit being, well, yellow!

Cautions: While Yellow Passionfruit is generally considered safe for consumption, parts of the plant, such as the leaves and stems, can contain cyanogenic glycosides. When ingested, these compounds may release cyanide, so exercise caution when handling the plant and avoid consuming any parts other than the ripe fruit.

Culinary Preparations: The delectable pulp of Yellow Passionfruit is a culinary delight, perfect for adding a burst of tropical flavor to smoothies, fruit salads, desserts, or even cocktails. The fruit can be eaten fresh, used as a topping, or blended into a variety of dishes, offering a tangy, sweet, and slightly tart taste sensation.

Medicinal Uses: Traditionally, Yellow Passionfruit has been used to treat various ailments, such as insomnia, anxiety, and digestive issues. Modern research has also found that the fruit is rich in antioxidants, vitamins, and minerals, which can contribute to overall health and well-being.

Fun or Historical Fact: Yellow Passionfruit was first introduced to the United States in the early 20th century. It quickly gained popularity in subtropical regions like Florida, where it thrives in warm climates.

Dog Toxicity: Keep your pup away from this one. Dogs may experience adverse reactions if they consume the plant's fruit, leaves, or stems. Symptoms of dog toxicity can include vomiting, diarrhea, abdominal pain, weakness, rapid breathing, and dilated pupils.

Yaupon Holly
Ilex vomitoria [EYE-LEKS VOM-IH-TOR-EE-UH]

Yaupon Holly is a versatile plant belonging to the Aquifoliaceae family. This enchanting evergreen goes by other delightful names such as Cassina, Christmas Berry, or Yaupon Tea. Yaupon Holly has been cherished for centuries, not only for its ornamental beauty but also for its stimulating, caffeinated leaves.

Location: Yaupon Holly is a proud native of the southeastern United States, including Texas, where you'll find it thriving in the eastern and coastal regions. This hardy plant is adaptable to various environments, from sandy dunes and coastal woodlands to stream banks and swamps.

Identification:

GROWTH/SIZE: A versatile, evergreen shrub or small tree that typically reaches heights of 30-40 feet. Its dense, rounded crown creates a beautiful silhouette in the landscape.

Bark/Stem/Root: The bark is smooth and gray, while the stems and roots are slender and woody, providing a solid framework for the plant's vibrant foliage.

Leaf: Each glossy, dark green leaf measures about 1/2-1 1/2 inches long, with slightly toothed margins and a leathery texture.

Flower: It dons small, inconspicuous white flowers in the spring. Each bloom measures approximately 1/4 inch in diameter and is usually found in clusters.

Fruit/Seed/Nut: The fruits are small, bright red berries that measure about 1/4 inch in diameter. These eye-catching berries are a feast for the eyes and a favorite food source for many bird species.

Look-A-Like Plants: Yaupon Holly can be easily confused with other holly species (*Ilex* spp.), such as **American Holly** (*Ilex opaca*). However, the smaller, toothed leaves and red berries of Yaupon Holly help distinguish it from other holly species, which are generally non-toxic.

Cautions: While Yaupon Holly's leaves are safe for human consumption, its berries can cause digestive upset if ingested.

Culinary Preparations: Yaupon Holly's claim to fame lies in its leaves, which can be used to create a stimulating, caffeinated tea. Roast the leaves, then steep them in hot water to make a delicious, energizing beverage that's been enjoyed for centuries.

Medicinal Uses: Traditionally, Yaupon Holly tea was consumed by Native Americans for its stimulating and purgative properties. Today, Yaupon tea is touted for its antioxidants, anti-inflammatory properties, and natural caffeine content, making it a popular alternative to coffee and other caffeinated beverages.

Fun or Historical Fact: Yaupon Holly's Latin name, *Ilex vomitoria*, comes from the Native American ritual called the "Black Drink Ceremony." The leaves were brewed into a strong tea, which was then consumed in large quantities to induce vomiting as a means of purification.

Dog Toxicity: Yaupon Holly berries can be toxic to dogs if ingested in large quantities, causing symptoms such as vomiting, diarrhea, and potentially more severe signs like seizures or coma.

PART FIVE
SAVORING THE LONE STAR STATE

A JOURNEY THROUGH TEXAS HERBS AND GRASSES

Blue Vervain

Verbena hastata [VER-BEE-NUH HA-STAY-TUH]

Blue Vervain is a fascinating herb belonging to the Verbenaceae family. Historically, it has been highly regarded for its medicinal properties and has been used across different cultures. The plant goes by other common names, such as Swamp Verbena, Wild Hyssop, and American Vervain.

Location: Native to North America, Blue Vervain can be found in various parts of the United States, including Texas. This adaptable plant is typically found in moist environments such as meadows, wetlands, and along the edges of streams and rivers.

Identification:

GROWTH/SIZE: Blue Vervain can grow up to 6 feet tall, making it a prominent feature in the landscapes where it's found.

Bark/Stem/Root: The plant has a square, slender, and branched stem covered in small hairs. The fibrous root system helps the plant anchor itself in its wet environment.

Leaf: The leaves are opposite, lance-shaped, and serrated, measuring 2 to 6 inches long. The leaves are attached to the stem by short petioles.

Flower: The showy blue to-violet flowers bloom from June to September, forming slender spikes reaching up to 8 inches. Each individual flower measures about 1/8 inch across.

Fruit/Seed/Nut: After flowering, Blue Vervain produces small, dry, nut-like fruits containing several seeds.

Look-A-Like Plants: **White Vervain** (*Verbena urticifolia*) is a non-toxic look-a-like plant that shares many characteristics with Blue Vervain. The primary difference is the color of the flowers, which are white or greenish-white in White Vervain.

Cautions: Blue Vervain is generally considered safe.

Culinary Preparations: Blue Vervain is not typically used in culinary preparations, as it tastes somewhat bitter. However, the leaves can be brewed into a tea for those who enjoy its flavor and potential health benefits.

Medicinal Uses: Traditionally, Blue Vervain has been used as a natural remedy for a variety of ailments, including anxiety, insomnia, and digestive issues. It has also been used as an expectorant, diuretic, and anti-inflammatory agent.

Fun or Historical Fact: In ancient Roman and Greek mythology, Blue Vervain was considered a sacred herb associated with the divine and often used in purification rituals.

Dog Toxicity: Blue Vervain is not considered toxic to dogs. If your dog shows signs of distress, such as vomiting, diarrhea, or lethargy, after consuming any part of a Blue Vervain plant, consult your veterinarian.

B roadleaf Cattail

Typha latifolia [TIE-ᴛᴜʜ ʟᴜʜ-TIFF-ᴏʜ-ʟᴇᴇ-ᴜʜ]

Broadleaf Cattail belongs to the Typhaceae family and has been a valuable resource for various cultures throughout history. With its distinctive appearance and multiple uses, it's no wonder that it has earned other familiar names like Bulrush, Great Reedmace, and Marsh Beetle. Native Americans and other cultures have utilized cattails for food, shelter, and even making boats.

Location: It's native to North America and can be found throughout the United States, including Texas. This versatile plant thrives in wetlands, marshes, swamps, and along the edges of ponds and lakes.

Identification:

Gʀᴏᴡᴛʜ/Sɪᴢᴇ: It can grow up to 10 feet tall, making it an easily identifiable plant in wetland areas.

Bark/Stem/Root: The plant's stem is round, smooth, and unbranched, while its extensive root system, called rhizomes, can spread rapidly in suitable conditions.

Leaf: It has long, flat, and linear leaves that can reach 3 to 10 feet long. The leaves are usually about 1 inch wide and light green.

Flower: Cattails are monoecious, meaning they have both male and female flowers on the same plant. The cylindrical, brown, sausage-like female flowers are what give the plant its distinctive appearance. The male flowers are yellowish and are located just above the female flowers. They bloom from late spring to early summer.

Fruit/Seed/Nut: After pollination, the female flower develops into a dense mass of tiny, fluffy seeds dispersed by wind and water.

Look-a-like(s): Narrowleaf Cattail (*Typha angustifolia*) is a non-toxic look-a-like plant that shares many similarities with Broadleaf Cattail. The main difference is in the leaves, which are narrower and more delicate in the Narrowleaf Cattail.

Cautions: Cattails are generally considered safe, but harvesting them from clean water sources is essential, as they can absorb pollutants and chemicals from their environment.

Culinary Preparations: Broadleaf Cattail offers multiple edible parts throughout the year. The young shoots can be eaten raw or cooked, the pollen can be collected and used as a flour substitute, and the rhizomes can be processed to extract starch. The young flower spikes can also be boiled and consumed like corn on the cob.

Medicinal Uses: Traditionally, the Broadleaf Cattail has been used to treat burns, wounds, and insect bites, thanks to its antiseptic properties. The downy seeds have been used as insulation material and can be applied to keep wounds clean and dry.

Fun or Historical Fact: Cattails have been called "the supermarket of the swamps" because of their wide range of uses, from food to shelter and even as a fuel source.

Dog Toxicity: Broadleaf Cattail is not considered toxic to dogs.

Evening Primrose

Oenothera biennis [EE-NO-THEE-ruh bye-EN-iss]

Evening Primrose, a plant from the Onagraceae family, has a rich history. It's known as Common Evening Primrose, Night Willow-Herb, and King's Cure-All. Indigenous peoples of North America have long recognized its medicinal and nutritional properties.

Location: It's native to North America and can be found across the United States, including Texas. It grows in a variety of habitats, such as roadsides, meadows, waste areas, and disturbed sites, preferring well-drained soils and sunny locations.

Identification:

GROWTH / SIZE: A biennial plant that grows from 1 to 5 feet tall with a sturdy, upright stem.

BARK / STEM / ROOT: The stem is green to reddish-green and slightly hairy, while the root system is a long taproot.

LEAF: Leaves are lance-shaped and measure 2 to 6 inches long and 1/2 to 1 1/2 inches wide. They have a slightly toothed margin and are arranged in a rosette during the first year of growth.

FLOWER: It produces beautiful, yellow, four-petaled flowers that measure 1 to 2 inches across. They bloom in the evening and close by late morning, attracting night-flying pollinators like moths.

FRUIT/SEED/NUT: It produces small, elongated seed capsules approximately 1 to 2 inches long. When mature, they release numerous tiny seeds.

Look-A-Like Plants: Evening Primrose might be confused with **Sundrops** (*Oenothera fruticosa*) or **Yellow Hawkweed** (*Hieracium caespitosum*), but these plants are non-toxic and generally considered safe.

Cautions: Evening Primrose is generally safe, but some people may experience mild gastrointestinal symptoms or headaches when ingesting the plant or its oil.

Culinary Preparations: The young leaves, flowers, and roots can be eaten raw or cooked. The leaves are often added to salads, while the roots can be boiled like potatoes. The seeds can produce Evening Primrose oil, which is rich in essential fatty acids.

Medicinal Uses: Traditionally, it has been used to treat a variety of ailments, including skin conditions, premenstrual syndrome, and gastrointestinal disorders. Modern research supports its use for some skin conditions, and its oil is a popular supplement for promoting overall health.

Fun or Historical Fact: Evening Primrose is sometimes called the "Cinderella of the Plant World" due to its enchanting transformation from a humble daytime appearance to a stunningly beautiful bloom that opens in the evening.

Dog Toxicity: Evening Primrose is not known to be toxic to dogs. If your dog shows symptoms like vomiting, diarrhea, or loss of appetite after consuming Evening Primrose, consult your veterinarian for guidance.

Greater Mullein

Verbascum thapsus [ver-BAS-kum THAP-sus]

Greater Mullein is a fascinating plant from the Scrophulariaceae family. It goes by several other common names, such as Common Mullein, Aaron's Rod, and Cowboy Toilet Paper. This plant has a long history of use in traditional medicine and for various practical purposes like candle wicks and torches.

Location: It's originally native to Europe, Asia, and northern Africa but has naturalized throughout North America, including Texas. It grows in various habitats, such as fields, pastures, roadsides, and disturbed areas, where it thrives in well-drained, sandy, and gravelly soils.

Identification:

Growth/Size: A biennial plant that grows a rosette of leaves in the first year and produces a flowering stalk in the second year. It can reach heights of 2 to 8 feet.

BARK/STEM/ROOT: The central stem is thick, strong, and covered with dense, woolly hairs. The root system consists of a long taproot.

LEAF: Its leaves are large, up to 20 inches long, and 5 inches wide. They are grayish-green, with a velvety texture due to the presence of soft, woolly hairs on both sides.

FLOWER: The flowers are yellow and about 1 inch in diameter. They bloom from June to September in dense, elongated clusters along the upper part of the flowering stalk.

FRUIT/SEED/NUT: Small, round capsules containing numerous tiny seeds develop after flowering. Each plant can produce up to 100,000 seeds.

Look-A-Like Plants: There are no significantly toxic look-alikes for Common Mullein. However, other species of Verbascum, such as **Moth Mullein** (*Verbascum blattaria*), have similar appearances but lack the dense, woolly hairs on their leaves.

Cautions: While Common Mullein is considered safe for most people, the hairs on the leaves can be irritating to some individuals, especially those with sensitive skin.

Culinary Preparations: Though it's not known for its culinary uses, the flowers can be used to make a mild, soothing tea, but it is primarily used for their medicinal properties.

Medicinal Uses: Historically, Greater Mullein has been used to remedy respiratory issues like coughs, colds, and bronchitis. The leaves and flowers can be made into tea, tincture, or syrup. Additionally, it has been employed as an anti-inflammatory, pain reliever, and wound healer.

Fun or Historical Fact: It was once called the "Candlewick Plant" because its dried stalks were dipped in tallow and used as torches or candle wicks in ancient times.

Dog Toxicity: There is no evidence to suggest that Common Mullein is toxic to dogs.

H orsemint

Monarda citriodora [MUH-NAR-DUH SIT-REE-UH-DAWR-UH]

Horsemint, a member of the Lamiaceae family, is a fascinating plant with a long history of use. It goes by other common names such as Spotted Beebalm, Dotted Mint, and Spotted Horsemint. Native American tribes have traditionally used this plant for its medicinal properties and as a flavoring agent.

Location: Horsemint is native to Texas and can be found throughout the state, particularly in the eastern, central, and southern regions. It grows in various habitats, including prairies, woodlands, and sandy soils, and thrives in sunny, well-drained areas.

Identification:

GROWTH/SIZE: Horsemint is a perennial plant that grows between 1 and 3 feet tall, with an upright, branched stem.

Bark/Stem/Root: The stem is square, a characteristic of the mint family, and is covered in fine hairs.

Leaf: Leaves are lance-shaped to ovate, measuring 1 to 3 inches long and 0.5 to 1.5 inches wide. They have serrated edges and are oppositely arranged along the stem.

Flower: The flowers are tubular and spotted, with colors ranging from yellow to purple or pink. They form dense, tiered whorls at the top of the plant and measure approximately 1 to 1.5 inches in diameter.

Fruit/Seed/Nut: It produces tiny, brown, nut-like fruits called nutlets, which are about 0.1 inches in size and contain seeds for reproduction.

Look-A-Like Plants: Horsemint may be confused with other plants from the mint family, such as **Wild Bergamot** (*Monarda fistulosa*) or **Lemon Mint** (*Monarda citriodora*). These plants are also non-toxic and have similar uses.

Cautions: Horsemint is generally considered safe when consumed in moderation.

Culinary Preparations: The leaves can be used as a culinary herb to flavor dishes or steeped as a refreshing herbal tea. The flowers are edible and can add a touch of color and flavor to salads.

Medicinal Uses: Traditionally, Horsemint has been used to treat digestive issues, colds, and respiratory infections. Its natural antiseptic properties make it useful for topical applications on minor skin irritations. Modern research is still investigating the full range of potential benefits.

Fun or Historical Fact: Horsemint attracts pollinators like bees, butterflies, and hummingbirds, making it a popular choice for gardeners looking to support local ecosystems and create a lively, buzzing garden.

Dog Toxicity: Horsemint is not known to be toxic to dogs. However, keeping your pets away from wild plants is always a good idea. If your dog shows symptoms like vomiting, diarrhea, or loss of appetite after consuming Horsemint, consult your veterinarian for guidance.

Inland Sea Oats

Chasmanthium latifolium [KAZ-MAN-THEE-UM LUH-TIF-OH-LEE-UHM]

Inland Sea Oats is a member of the Poaceae family. This attractive grass is also commonly referred to as Northern Sea Oats, Broadleaf Woodoats, or Indian Woodoats. Its original use was primarily ornamental, and Native Americans also utilized the seeds as a food source.

Location: Inland Sea Oats are native to the southeastern United States, including the eastern and central regions of Texas. It grows in a variety of habitats, such as woodlands, riverbanks, and shady slopes, where it enjoys moist, well-drained soils and partial to full shade.

Identification:

GROWTH / SIZE: A perennial grass typically grows between 2 and 4 feet tall.

BARK / STEM / ROOT: The plant has slender, arching stems, which are green during the growing season and turn a coppery brown in the fall.

Leaf: The leaves are broad and flat, measuring approximately 8 to 10 inches long and 1 to 2 inches wide. They are green during the growing season and change to a golden brown hue in the fall.

Flower: It produces distinctive, oat-like seed heads that hang in clusters from the arching stems. The seed heads are approximately 1 to 2 inches long and turn from green to golden brown as they mature.

Fruit/Seed/Nut: The fruit consists of small, flat, oval seeds that develop within the drooping seed heads.

Look-A-Like(s): Inland Sea Oats might be confused with other ornamental grasses, but their distinctive, drooping seed heads make them relatively easy to identify. There are no known toxic look-a-like plants.

Caution(s): There are no known cautions.

Culinary Preparations: Inland Sea Oats seeds can be eaten either raw or cooked. The seeds can be ground into flour and used in bread or other baked goods.

Medicinal Uses: There are no well-known medicinal uses for Inland Sea Oats.

Fun or Historical Fact: Inland Sea Oats are a popular choice for landscaping, especially in shaded areas, due to their beautiful appearance and ability to prevent soil erosion, making them an excellent option for stabilizing slopes and riverbanks.

Dog Toxicity: Inland Sea Oats are not known to be toxic to dogs.

I ndian Ricegrass

Achnatherum hymenoides [AK-NUH-THEER-UM HI-MEN-OY-DEEZ]

Indian ricegrass is a perennial bunchgrass that belongs to the Poaceae family. This intriguing plant has played a significant role in the lives of Native American tribes who referred to it by other names such as sand ricegrass and Indian millet. Its seeds were an essential food source for these tribes, providing them with a nutritious and versatile grain.

Location: Indian ricegrass is native to the western United States, including Texas. It's commonly found in arid regions such as deserts, sandy soils, and dry grasslands, where it thrives in challenging conditions.

Identification:

GROWTH/SIZE: It typically grows between 1 to 2 feet tall, with a similar spread, creating a dense and beautiful bunch.

Bark/Stem/Root: It has slender, wiry stems that are strong and well-adapted to its arid environment. Its fibrous roots extend deep into the ground to access water and nutrients.

Leaf: The leaves are narrow, rolled, and usually between 4 to 12 inches long. They are typically green or blue-green and may become curly as they mature.

Flower: It produces delicate, feathery flowers between April and June. The flowers are clustered in open, airy panicles 3 to 8 inches long.

Fruit/Seed/Nut: The seeds are small, rice-like grains enclosed in a papery husk. They are highly nutritious and essential food sources for indigenous people and wildlife.

Look-A-Like Plants: Indian ricegrass is often confused with **needle-and-thread grass** (*Hesperostipa comata*), another non-toxic grass species. The main difference between the two is the seed head; needle-and-thread grass has a longer awn than Indian ricegrass.

Cautions: Indian ricegrass is considered safe for consumption.

Culinary Preparations: The seeds can be ground into flour and used in various dishes, such as bread, pancakes, and porridge. The grains can also be cooked and eaten whole, similar to rice or quinoa.

Medicinal Uses: While not widely known for its medicinal properties, Indian ricegrass has been used traditionally to soothe digestive issues and promote overall health due to its high nutritional value.

Fun or Historical Fact: Indian ricegrass was so valuable to Native American tribes that they would cultivate and manage the plants to ensure a sustainable harvest.

Dog Toxicity: Indian ricegrass is not considered toxic to dogs.

S potted Joe-Pye Weed

Eutrochium maculatum [YOO-TROH-KEE-UM MAK-YOO-LAY-TUM]

Joe-Pye Weed, a member of the Asteraceae family, has a rich history of use in traditional medicine. It is known as Gravel Root, Sweet Joe-Pye Weed, or Purple Boneset. Native American tribes, particularly the Algonquin, used the plant to treat various ailments, and it is even named after a Native American healer named Joe Pye.

Location: Joe-Pye Weed is native to eastern North America and can be found in the eastern and central regions of Texas. It grows in a variety of habitats, such as moist meadows, wetlands, and woodland edges, preferring damp, well-drained soils and partial to full sunlight.

Identification:

GROWTH/SIZE: A tall, herbaceous perennial, growing between 4 and 7 feet in height, depending on the conditions.

Bark/Stem/Root: The stem is sturdy and upright, with a reddish-purple hue, and may be spotted or streaked. The plant produces thick, fibrous roots.

Leaf: it has large, lance-shaped leaves measuring 4 to 12 inches long and 1.5 to 4 inches wide. The leaves are arranged in whorls of 3 to 6 around the stem, with serrated margins and a dark green color.

Flower: The flowers form large, domed clusters at the top of the plant, with each cluster measuring 4 to 7 inches in diameter. The individual flowers are small, sweet-scented, and pink to purple.

Fruit/Seed/Nut: It produces tiny, brown, dry fruits called achenes, each containing a single seed for reproduction.

Look-A-Like Plants: Joe-Pye Weed may be confused with other tall, flowering plants in the Asteraceae family, such as **Boneset** (*Eupatorium perfoliatum*) or **Ironweed** (*Vernonia spp.*). These plants are generally non-toxic and have similar uses.

Cautions: Joe-Pye Weed is considered safe when used correctly.

Culinary Preparations: While not commonly used in culinary preparations, Joe-Pye Weed's young leaves and shoots can be consumed in moderation when cooked.

Medicinal Uses: Historically, it has been used to treat kidney stones, urinary tract infections, and other ailments. Modern research is still exploring the full range of potential benefits, but it has been used in herbal medicine to support kidney and urinary health.

Fun or Historical Fact: The sweet-scented flowers of Joe-Pye Weed are attractive to butterflies and other pollinators, making them an excellent addition to pollinator-friendly gardens.

Dog Toxicity: Joe-Pye Weed is not known to be toxic to dogs.

Lemon Balm

Melissa officinalis [MUH-LIS-uh uh-FUH-SUH-NA-lis]

Lemon balm has a long history of medicinal and culinary herb use. A member of the Lamiaceae family, this aromatic plant goes by other common names such as Bee Balm, Sweet Balm, or simply Balm. Since ancient times, people have cherished lemon balm for its calming effects, delightful fragrance, and delicate flavor.

Location: Originally native to the Mediterranean region and parts of Asia, lemon balm is now widely cultivated and naturalized worldwide. In Texas, it can be found growing in gardens, along roadsides, or in abandoned fields, thriving in both full sun and partial shade. Lemon balm prefers well-drained soils and can tolerate a range of conditions.

Identification:

GROWTH/SIZE: A perennial herb, typically growing between 12 and 32 inches tall.

Bark/Stem/Root: The plant features square, slightly hairy stems with a light green to reddish-brown color. It has a fibrous root system.

Leaf: Lemon balm leaves are oval, measuring 0.8 to 2.4 inches long and 0.6 to 1.8 inches wide, with a wrinkled texture and serrated edges. The leaves are bright green and emit a lovely lemon scent when crushed.

Flower: The flowers are small, tubular, and white to pale yellow with a touch of purple. They appear in clusters at the leaf axils between June and September.

Fruit/Seed/Nut: It produces small, brown, dry, and roundish nutlets containing seeds for reproduction.

Look-A-Like Plants: Lemon balm could be confused with other plants in the Lamiaceae family, such as mint species (Mentha spp.) or **Catnip** (*Nepeta cataria*). These plants are generally non-toxic and have similar uses.

Cautions: Lemon balm is generally considered safe, but allergic reactions are rare and can occur in some individuals.

Culinary Preparations: Lemon balm is a versatile herb in the kitchen, lending its lemony flavor to teas, salads, sauces, and desserts. Its fresh leaves can be added to dishes, while the dried leaves can be used for making herbal teas.

Medicinal Uses: Traditionally, lemon balm has been used to soothe anxiety, stress, and insomnia. It also has antiviral properties and is used to treat cold sores. Modern research supports the calming effects of lemon balm, and it's often used in herbal remedies for relaxation and sleep support.

Fun or Historical Fact: Lemon balm was so highly regarded in ancient times that the famous Greek physician Dioscorides recommended it for treating "all complaints supposed to proceed from a disordered state of the nervous system."

Dog Toxicity: Lemon balm is not known to be toxic to dogs.

Mexican Oregano

Lippia graveolens [LIP-ee-uh gruh-VEE-oh-lenz]

Mexican oregano, or Lippia graveolens, has a rich history as a beloved culinary and medicinal herb. It belongs to the Verbenaceae family and is distinct from the more familiar Mediterranean oregano, a Lamiaceae family member. Other common names for Mexican oregano include Redbrush Lippia and Oregano Cimarrón. This potent herb has traditionally been used in Mexican cuisine as a folk remedy for various ailments.

Location: It's native to Mexico, Central America, and parts of the southwestern United States, including Texas. It thrives in sunny, arid regions and grows in rocky or sandy soils, along roadsides, and in desert scrublands.

Identification:

GROWTH / SIZE: A perennial shrub typically grows between 3 and 6 feet tall.

BARK / STEM / ROOT: The plant has woody, branched stems with a light gray to reddish-brown color. It features a fibrous and shallow root system.

Leaf: The leaves are simple, opposite, and lanceolate, measuring approximately 0.8 to 2 inches long and 0.3 to 0.7 inches wide. They have a rough texture and dark green color and emit a strong, aromatic scent when crushed.

Flower: It produces small, tubular, white to pale pink flowers in dense clusters at the tips of the branches. Blooming occurs from summer to early fall.

Fruit/Seed/Nut: The fruit is a small, dry, brownish nutlet containing the plant's seeds.

Look-A-Like Plants: Mexican oregano can be confused with other Lippia genus species or **Mediterranean oregano** (*Origanum vulgare*). However, these plants are generally non-toxic and have similar culinary and medicinal uses.

Cautions: Mexican oregano is generally considered safe for culinary use, but allergic reactions are rare, and they can occur in some individuals.

Culinary Preparations: Mexican oregano is a popular ingredient in Mexican and Tex-Mex cuisines, where its robust flavor enhances dishes such as chili, enchiladas, and salsas. It can be used fresh or dried, and its leaves are often ground into a powder for easy storage and use.

Medicinal Uses: Traditionally, Mexican oregano has been used to treat respiratory infections, digestive issues, and skin ailments. Modern research has shown that the herb possesses antimicrobial, antioxidant, and anti-inflammatory properties, which may support its traditional uses.

Fun or Historical Fact: Mexican oregano was highly valued by the Aztecs, who used it not only as a seasoning but also as a preservative and a remedy for a variety of ailments.

Dog Toxicity: Mexican oregano is not known to be toxic to dogs.

Purple Coneflower

Echinacea purpurea [EH-KUH-NAY-SHUH PURR-PUR-EE-UH]

Echinacea, a popular plant from the Asteraceae family, has a fascinating history. It's also known as Echinacea, Eastern Purple Coneflower, and Hedgehog Coneflower. Echinacea has been used for centuries by Native American tribes for its powerful medicinal properties.

Location: Native to central and eastern North America, including Texas, Echinacea can be found in prairies, meadows, and open woodlands. It prefers well-drained, loamy soils and thrives in full sun to partial shade.

Identification:

GROWTH / SIZE: A perennial plant that grows from 1.5 to 5 feet tall, producing strong, upright stems.

BARK / STEM / ROOT: The stems are green and slightly hairy, while the root system is fibrous and thick.

LEAF: The leaves are lance-shaped, measuring 4 to 8 inches long and 1 to 2 inches wide. They have a rough texture and toothed margins.

FLOWER: The striking flowers are 3 to 4 inches across, with a prominent central cone surrounded by drooping, purple-pink petals. They bloom from mid-summer to early fall.

FRUIT/SEED/NUT: It produces small, elongated, dry seeds that are dispersed by the wind once the flower head dries.

Look-A-Like Plants: Echinacea may be confused with other coneflowers like **Pale Purple Coneflower** (*Echinacea pallida*) or **Yellow Coneflower** (*Ratibida pinnata*), but these plants are not toxic and also have medicinal properties.

Cautions: Echinacea is generally safe, but some people may experience allergic reactions or gastrointestinal upset. Use caution if you have a known allergy to plants in the Asteraceae family or a compromised immune system.

Culinary Preparations: Echinacea is not typically used in culinary applications, as it is primarily valued for its medicinal properties.

Medicinal Uses: Traditionally, Echinacea has been used to boost the immune system and help fight off infections, such as colds and the flu. It has also been employed as an anti-inflammatory and wound healer. Modern research supports its use for immune system support, and it is commonly found in teas, tinctures, and supplements.

Fun or Historical Fact: Native American tribes, such as the Plains Indians, used Echinacea to treat a wide range of ailments, including toothaches and snakebites, and even as a painkiller during childbirth.

Dog Toxicity: Echinacea is not known to be toxic to dogs.

R osemary
Salvia rosmarinus [SAL-VEE-UH ROH-ZUH-MAR-IN-US]

Rosemary is an aromatic, evergreen shrub that belongs to the Lamiaceae family. It has been a popular herb for centuries, known for its unique fragrance and flavor. Rosemary is also called compass-weed, polar plant, and elf leaf, among other names. It was traditionally used for various purposes, such as culinary, medicinal, and even spiritual.

Location: Rosemary is native to the Mediterranean region but has found a welcoming home in Texas. It is well-adapted to the state's warm climate and can be found thriving in gardens, landscapes, and even some wild areas.

Identification:

GROWTH/SIZE: A woody, perennial shrub that can grow between 2 to 6 feet tall, depending on the variety and growing conditions.

Bark/Stem/Root: The plant has a fibrous root system and woody stems that become thicker and more twisted as the plant ages. The stems are usually covered with thin, flaky bark.

Leaf: Rosemary's leaves are needle-like, about 1 to 2 inches long, and have a dark green upper surface with a silvery-white underside. The leaves are rich in aromatic oils that give the plant its characteristic fragrance.

Flower: It produces small, tubular flowers, usually blue to purple, that appear between late winter and early spring. The flowers are about 0.3 to 0.5 inches long and attract bees and other pollinators.

Fruit/Seed/Nut: Rosemary produces no significant fruit, seed, or nut. It is primarily propagated through cuttings.

Look-A-Like Plants: Bog rosemary (*Andromeda polifolia*) is a non-toxic plant that resembles rosemary due to its needle-like leaves. However, bog rosemary is found in wet, acidic habitats, while rosemary prefers well-drained, sunnier locations.

Cautions: Rosemary is generally safe for consumption, but pregnant women should avoid consuming large amounts of rosemary, as it may stimulate uterine contractions.

Culinary Preparations: Rosemary is a versatile herb used in various dishes, such as roasted meats, vegetables, and soups. It can also be infused with oils or used as a seasoning in bread and other baked goods.

Medicinal Uses: Traditionally, rosemary was used to improve memory, alleviate digestive issues, and reduce inflammation. Modern research has found that it contains antioxidants and antimicrobial properties, which support its traditional uses.

Fun or Historical Fact: In ancient Greece, students wore rosemary garlands while studying, which was believed to enhance memory and concentration.

Dog Toxicity: Rosemary is not considered toxic to dogs.

Y arrow

Achillea millefolium [AH-KIH-LEE-UH MIL-UH-FOH-LEE-UHM]

Yarrow is a member of the Asteraceae family and has been cherished for its medicinal properties since ancient times. This hardy perennial is also known as Soldier's Woundwort, Bloodwort, and Thousand-Leaf, among other names. Yarrow's original use dates back to ancient Greece, where it was utilized to treat wounds, hence its association with Achilles, the legendary Greek hero.

Location: Yarrow is native to Europe and Asia but has become naturalized in many parts of North America, including Texas. It can be found growing in various habitats, such as meadows, grasslands, and along roadsides, preferring well-drained soil and sunny conditions.

Identification:

GROWTH/SIZE: A perennial plant that grows between 1 and 3 feet tall. Its growth habit is upright and tends to spread via rhizomes and self-seeding.

Bark/Stem/Root: The plant has slender, grooved, and erect stems that are mostly green but may have a reddish tinge, especially near the base.

Leaf: The leaves are finely dissected, giving them a feathery, lace-like appearance. They measure between 2 and 8 inches in length, are green to grayish-green, and have a slightly aromatic scent when crushed.

Flower: The flowers are small, usually white or pale pink, and clustered together in flat-topped, umbrella-like arrays. Flowering typically occurs from spring to fall.

Fruit/Seed/Nut: After flowering, it produces tiny, brown, oblong-shaped fruits containing small, lightweight seeds.

Look-A-Like Plants: Yarrow can be confused with other plants in the carrot family, such as Queen Anne's Lace or Hemlock. Be cautious when identifying Yarrow, as Hemlock is highly toxic.

Cautions: Yarrow is generally considered safe for external and moderate internal use. Pregnant or breastfeeding women should also avoid consuming Yarrow due to potential uterine-stimulating effects.

Culinary Preparations: Yarrow can be used as a culinary herb, adding a mild, aromatic flavor to dishes. The young leaves can be added to salads or cooked as a vegetable, while the flowers can be used to make tea or as a garnish.

Medicinal Uses: Traditionally, Yarrow has been used to treat wounds, stop bleeding and reduce inflammation. Modern research suggests that Yarrow possesses antimicrobial, anti-inflammatory, and antioxidant properties, supporting its historical uses. It's also been used to treat digestive issues, fevers, and menstrual discomfort.

Fun or Historical Fact: Yarrow has been found in ancient burial sites, suggesting its importance in medicinal and spiritual practices throughout history. It was also used as a divination tool for love and in rituals for protection.

Dog Toxicity: Yarrow is not known to be toxic to dogs.

Western Wheatgrass

Pascopyrum smithii [PAS-KO-PI-RUM SMITH-EE-EYE]

Western Wheatgrass is a perennial grass belonging to the Poaceae family. Known for its resilience and adaptability, this grass is also called bluejoint wheatgrass, western couchgrass, and Colorado wheatgrass. Western wheatgrass has been valued for its ability to stabilize soil, provide forage for livestock, and serve as a food source.

Location: Western wheatgrass is native to the western United States, including Texas. It thrives in various habitats, such as prairies, grasslands, and plains, and can be found along stream banks, ditches, and disturbed areas.

Identification:

GROWTH/SIZE: Western wheatgrass typically grows 1 to 3 feet tall, forming dense clumps or sods.

Bark/Stem/Root: This grass has a creeping rhizomatous root system, allowing it to spread efficiently and stabilize the soil. The stems are erect, slender, and usually unbranched.

Leaf: The leaves are long, narrow, and flat, measuring 4 to 12 inches long. They can have a blue-green to grayish-green hue.

Flower: Western wheatgrass produces spike-like flower panicles 2 to 6 inches long, containing tightly packed spikelets along the central axis.

Fruit/Seed/Nut: The seeds are small, elongated, and brownish, enclosed within the spikelets of the flower panicle.

Look-A-Like Plants: Western wheatgrass may resemble other grass species, such as **Crested wheatgrass** (*Agropyron cristatum*) or **Blue grama** (*Bouteloua gracilis*). Examining the flower panicle and leaf characteristics can help differentiate between these species.

Cautions: Western wheatgrass is generally considered safe.

Culinary Preparations: The seeds can be ground into flour, used in baking, or added to dishes as a whole grain, similar to quinoa or millet. Native Americans have used the seeds to make porridge or flatbread.

Medicinal Uses: While not widely known for its medicinal properties, western wheatgrass has been used traditionally as a food source to maintain overall health and well-being due to its nutritional content.

Fun or Historical Fact: Western wheatgrass was designated the state grass of Montana in 1973, reflecting its importance as a forage grass and soil stabilizer.

Dog Toxicity: Western wheatgrass is not known to be toxic to dogs.

PAY IT FORWARD...

"The greatest gifts are not wrapped in paper but in love and the beauty of nature." - Anonymous.

Picture this: someone's standing in the middle of the wilderness, surrounded by the raw beauty of nature. But there's a tiny hiccup - they're a tad unsure which of the green wonders before them might serve as a delicious snack or which might send them on an unplanned trip to the ER. Now, what if YOUR review could be the deciding factor that guides them on this journey? How many times have we relied on the experiences of others before diving into a new adventure? Countless, right? How gratifying does it feel when we can be that guiding light for someone else?

Leaving a review isn't just a simple clickety-clack of your keyboard. Nope! It's a chance to share your wisdom, your "Ah-ha!" moments, and even your "Oops, shouldn't have eaten that" tales. By jotting down your thoughts, you're crafting a lighthouse for fellow enthusiasts, helping them navigate the vast ocean of edible greens.

Why We Need YOU!

In this digital age, there's an overabundance of information, but what's truly precious? Genuine experiences. Your insights are invaluable. By leaving an honest review, you ensure others get the most out of their edible journey without the pitfalls. Remember, your words could be the compass someone else is desperately seeking.

We're reaching out with a heartfelt plea: could you spare a few moments to leave an honest review? Your words will be the torch that lights up another enthusiast's path.

How to Review:

Just scan the QR code below:

Pour your heart out! Let us know what you loved and learned and any tips you might have.

Hit "Submit," and voilà, the review is done! It only takes 30 seconds to help others benefit.

The Ripple Effect

Every keystroke, every word, creates a ripple. By sharing your experiences, you're not just adding to a digital platform but making a real, tangible impact in someone's life. Your review could catalyze someone's passion or help a novice avoid a potentially prickly situation.

Happy Foraging,

Shannon Warner

PART SIX

TEXAS TIMBER AND TASTY TREASURES

A FORAGER'S GUIDE TO THE NUTTY WONDERS OF THE LONE STAR STATE

B lack Hickory
Carya texana [KAIR-EE-UH TEK-SAY-NUH]

Black Hickory is a slow-growing, deciduous tree from the Juglandaceae family, known for its strong and durable wood. The tree also goes by names such as Texas Hickory and Buckley Hickory. Historically, wood was highly valued for making tool handles, furniture, and even wheels, thanks to its strength and resistance to wear.

Location: Native to Texas, Black Hickory is mainly found in the eastern and central parts of the state. This hardy tree can tolerate dry, rocky soils and is often found on limestone outcrops or well-drained slopes.

Identification:

GROWTH / SIZE: It can grow up to 50 to 75 feet tall with a trunk diameter of 1 to 2 feet.

Bark/Stem/Root: The bark is dark gray to black, with deep furrows and rough ridges forming a diamond-shaped pattern. The tree has a deep taproot, making it difficult to transplant.

Leaf: It has compound leaves that measure about 8 to 12 inches long, with 5 to 7 lanceolate, serrated leaflets per leaf. The leaflets are dark green on the upper surface and lighter on the lower surface.

Flower: The tree produces small, greenish-yellow, inconspicuous flowers in spring. Male flowers appear as catkins, while female flowers are short spikes.

Fruit/Seed/Nut: It produces round to slightly oblong nuts that measure about 1 to 1.5 inches in diameter. The nuts have a thick, hard shell and a small, sweet kernel.

Look-A-Like(s): Black Hickory can be confused with **Pignut Hickory** (*Carya glabra*), which has a similar bark pattern but lighter gray color. Pignut Hickory also has smaller nuts with thinner shells.

Cautions: There are no specific cautions related to Black Hickory.

Culinary Preparations: The sweet kernels of Black Hickory nuts can be eaten raw or used in various recipes, such as baked goods and candies.

Medicinal Uses: There are no well-documented medicinal uses for Black Hickory. However, the bark of other hickory species has been used in traditional medicine to treat ailments such as arthritis and rheumatism.

A Fun or Historical Fact: Black Hickory wood was used by early American settlers to create long-lasting and durable wagon wheels, thanks to its strength and resistance to wear.

Dog Toxicity: Black Hickory is not known to be toxic to dogs. However, large nuts could pose a choking hazard for small dogs, so keep them out of reach.

Blackjack Oak

Quercus marilandica [KWUR-KUHS MUH-RIH-LAN-DIH-KUH]

Blackjack Oak is a Fagaceae family member known for its hardiness and ruggedness. Other common names are Barren Oak, Pin Oak, and Scrub Oak. Due to its dense and heavy wood, the tree has been traditionally used for fuelwood and charcoal production.

Location: Blackjack Oak is native to the southeastern United States, including Texas. In Texas, it primarily grows in the eastern and central parts of the state. It thrives in dry, sandy, or rocky soils and can often be found in upland areas, woodlands, and along forest edges.

Identification:

GROWTH/SIZE: A small to medium-sized tree, typically reaching 20 to 50 feet in height and 1 to 2 feet in diameter.

Bark/Stem/Root: The bark is dark, thick, and rough, with deep furrows and irregular ridges. The branches tend to be twisted, while the roots are shallow and well-adapted to dry infertile soils.

Leaf: The leaves are 4 to 8 inches long and 2 to 4 inches wide. They are shiny dark green on the upper surface, while the lower surface is paler and often has fine hairs. The leaves are characterized by their bell-shaped or triangular form with bristle-tipped lobes.

Flower: The tree produces male and female flowers on the same tree (monoecious). Male flowers appear as slender, drooping catkins, while female flowers are small and inconspicuous, usually occurring in small clusters.

Fruit/Seed/Nut: It produces acorns that are ½ to 1 inch in length. The acorns are brown to black, with a shallow, saucer-like cap covering only the nut's top portion.

Look-A-Like Plants: Blackjack Oak may be confused with other oak species like **Post Oak** (*Quercus stellata*) or **Water Oak** (*Quercus nigra*). However, the unique bell-shaped or triangular leaves of Blackjack Oak help distinguish it from other species.

Cautions: Acorns from Blackjack Oak, like those from other oak species, contain tannins that can be toxic if consumed in large quantities. Leaching the acorns in water is necessary to remove tannins before consumption.

Culinary Preparations: After leaching the acorns, they can be ground into flour and used in various recipes, such as bread, pancakes, or muffins. The acorns can also be roasted and used as a coffee substitute.

Medicinal Uses: Traditionally, the bark of the Blackjack Oak was used by Native Americans to treat various ailments, such as diarrhea and hemorrhoids. The bark's astringent properties were also used to treat wounds and inflammation.

Fun or Historical Fact: Blackjack Oak is a crucial tree for wildlife. The acorns provide a vital food source for various mammals, such as deer, squirrels, and wild turkeys. The tree's cavities also serve as nesting sites for birds like the Red-headed Woodpecker and Eastern Screech-Owl.

Dog Toxicity:

Common Hackberry

Celtis occidentalis [SELL-TISS OH-KIH-DEN-TUH-LIS]

Common Hackberry is a deciduous tree from the Cannabaceae family, known for its unique bark and hardy nature. Other names, such as Northern Hackberry or American Hackberry, also know it. Historically, the tree was valued for its wood, used in various construction projects and toolmaking.

Location: Native to Texas, it's found in the eastern and central parts of the state, often near streams or riverbanks. This adaptable tree also thrives in a variety of soil types and can tolerate urban environments.

Identification:

GROWTH/SIZE: Can grow up to 40 to 60 feet tall, with a canopy width of 30 to 50 feet.

BARK/STEM/ROOT: The bark is light gray to grayish-brown and features distinctive warty ridges that create a cork-like appearance. The stems are slender and smooth, while the root system is relatively shallow.

LEAF: The leaves are simple, alternate, and ovate, measuring about 2 to 4 inches long. They have serrated edges, a pointed tip, and a slightly rough texture on the upper surface.

FLOWER: It produces small, inconspicuous greenish flowers in spring. Each flower measures about 1/8 inch in diameter.

FRUIT/SEED/NUT: The tree produces small, round drupes that measure about 1/4 inch in diameter. These fruits are initially green, turning dark purple to black when ripe.

Look-A-Like Plants: Common Hackberry can be mistaken for **Sugarberry** (*Celtis laevigata*), which also belongs to the same genus. Sugarberry has smoother bark, and its leaves are more lanceolate in shape.

Cautions: No significant cautions are associated with the Common Hackberry, but always exercise care when handling trees or plants to avoid injury.

Culinary Preparations: While not commonly used in culinary preparations, the fruits are edible and can be consumed raw or used to make jellies.

Medicinal Uses: Historically, Native Americans used the bark and roots to treat sore throats and digestive issues. However, there is limited modern scientific evidence to support these uses.

A Fun or Historical Fact: The distinctive warty bark has led to its nickname, "the wart tree." This unique bark texture makes it an attractive tree for landscaping and ornamental purposes.

Dog Toxicity: Common Hackberry is not known to be toxic to dogs.

Edwards Plateau Pecan

Carya illinoinensis [KAIR-EE-UH IH-LUH-NOY-EN-SIS]

The Edwards Plateau Pecan is a variety of pecan trees native to the Edwards Plateau region of Texas. Belonging to the Juglandaceae (walnut) family, this tree is known for its delicious nuts, which have been enjoyed for centuries. Pecans have a rich history in Native American culture, with nuts being used as a valuable food source and wood for making tools.

Location: It's native to central Texas, where it can grow along the rivers and streams of the Edwards Plateau region. This pecan variety is adapted to the region's limestone-rich soils and can be found in mixed woodlands, bottomlands, and near water sources.

Identification:

GROWTH/SIZE: It can grow up to 70 feet tall and have a spreading canopy, providing ample shade in the landscape.

Bark/Stem/Root: The bark is gray to brown, with shallow furrows and scaly ridges. The branches are reddish-brown, and the tree has a deep taproot system that enables it to access water and nutrients.

Leaf: The leaves are pinnately compound and measure 12 to 20 inches long. Each leaf has 9 to 17 lance-shaped leaflets, which are dark green on the upper surface and paler green below.

Flower: They are monoecious, producing separate male and female flowers on the same tree. The male flowers are yellow-green catkins, measuring 3 to 6 inches long, while the female flowers are small, reddish-green, and located at the tips of branches.

Fruit/Seed/Nut: The fruit is a brown, oblong nut that measures about 1 to 2 inches long. The nuts have a thin shell filled with sweet, rich, buttery-flavored kernels.

Look-A-Like Plants: The Edwards Plateau Pecan is similar to other hickory species, such as the **Shagbark Hickory** (*Carya ovata*) and the **Shellbark Hickory** (*Carya laciniosa*). However, the distinctive oblong nuts of the pecan set it apart from its relatives.

Cautions: No significant cautions are associated with the Edwards Plateau Pecan tree.

Culinary Preparations: Pecans are widely used in cooking and baking for their rich, buttery flavor. They can be eaten raw or roasted, added to salads, pies, cakes, and cookies, or used to make pecan butter, oil, and flour.

Medicinal Uses: While not typically medicinal, pecans are rich in antioxidants, healthy fats, and essential nutrients. They may help support heart health, brain function, and overall wellness.

A Fun or Historical Fact: The word "pecan" comes from the Native American Algonquin word "paccan," which means "nut that requires a stone to crack." Pecans were an essential food source for Native Americans, and they taught early European settlers how to harvest and use nuts.

Dog Toxicity: Pecans themselves are not toxic to dogs. However, moldy pecans can produce a toxic compound called "aflatoxin," which can cause symptoms like vomiting, diarrhea, loss of appetite, and lethargy in dogs. Keeping your dog away from moldy pecans or any nuts stored in damp conditions is essential.

M esquite
Prosopis spp. [PROH-SOH-PIS]

Mesquite trees, part of the Fabaceae family, are a group of deciduous or semi-evergreen trees and shrubs known for their hardiness and versatility. The most common species include Honey mesquite (*Prosopis glandulosa*), Velvet mesquite (*Prosopis velutina*), and Screwbean mesquite (*Prosopis pubescens*). These trees have been used for centuries by indigenous peoples for food, medicine, and building materials.

Location: Mesquite trees are native to Texas and can be found across the state, particularly in the southern, central, and western regions. They thrive in arid environments and can adapt to a variety of soil types.

Identification:

GROWTH / SIZE: They can grow anywhere from 10 to 30 feet tall depending on the species and environmental conditions.

Bark/Stem/Root: The bark is rough and brown, with deep furrows and ridges. Their stems are often twisted, with many branches covered in sharp thorns that can be 1 to 3 inches long. Mesquite trees have an extensive root system that can reach depths of over 50 feet in search of water.

Leaf: The leaves are compound, featuring 6 to 30 pairs of small, oblong leaflets, each measuring about 0.5 to 1 inch long.

Flower: They produce small, tubular, and fragrant yellow-green flower clusters. Each flower is about 0.1 to 0.2 inches long.

Fruit/Seed/Nut: Mesquite trees bear elongated seed pods ranging from 2 to 8 inches in length. These pods are tan or reddish-brown and contain numerous small, hard seeds.

Look-A-Like Plants: Mesquite trees can be confused with other thorny trees or shrubs, such as acacia or palo verde. However, mesquite trees can be distinguished by their compound leaves, fragrant flowers, and elongated seed pods.

Cautions: Mesquite trees are generally safe, but their thorns can cause injuries. Be cautious when handling these trees to avoid being pricked.

Culinary Preparations: Mesquite pods are edible and can be ground into a nutritious, gluten-free flour used in baking or as a natural sweetener. Mesquite wood is also famous for smoking and barbecuing meats, imparting a unique flavor.

Medicinal Uses: Traditionally, Native Americans used different parts of the mesquite tree for medicinal purposes. The leaves were brewed into a tea to alleviate digestive issues, while the bark was used to treat wounds and skin infections.

A Fun or Historical Fact: Mesquite trees played an essential role in the lives of indigenous peoples, who utilized nearly every part of the tree. The wood was used for building and making tools, the roots for basket weaving, and the sap for making gum.

Dog Toxicity: Mesquite trees are not known to be toxic to dogs. However, ingesting large pods or seeds may cause gastrointestinal upset.

Osage Orange

Maclura pomifera [MUH-KLOOR-UH PUH-MIF-ER-UH]

The Osage Orange belongs to the Moraceae plant family, and it is commonly known by various names such as hedge apple, horse apple, bodark, and bois d'arc. Initially, the tree was valued for its durable, rot-resistant wood, which Native Americans and early settlers used for making hunting bows, hence the name "bois d'arc" (bow wood).

Location: Osage Orange is native to the south-central United States, including parts of Texas. It can be found in the eastern and central parts of the state. The tree grows well in a variety of soil types and can tolerate drought conditions.

Identification:

GROWTH/SIZE: It typically grows to 30-40 feet, with some specimens reaching up to 60 feet.

Bark/Stem/Root: The bark is thick, deeply furrowed, and orangish-brown. The branches often have long, stout thorns up to 2 inches long.

Leaf: The leaves are deciduous, simple, and alternate, measuring 3-5 inches long and 1-3 inches wide. They are lance-shaped with a pointed tip and have smooth margins.

Flower: The flowers are small and greenish-yellow, appearing in late spring. Male and female flowers grow on separate trees (dioecious).

Fruit/Seed/Nut: The fruit is a large, bumpy, and inedible green ball measuring up to 6 inches in diameter. The fruit contains a sticky, white latex-like substance and numerous seeds.

Look-A-Like Plants: There are no close look-a-like plants to the Osage Orange. Its distinctive fruit, thorny branches, and unique bark set it apart from other trees.

Cautions: While the fruit of the Osage Orange is not toxic, it is inedible and can cause stomach irritation if consumed. The fruit's milky sap can also cause skin irritation in some individuals. Avoid contact with the sap and thoroughly wash your hands if handling the fruit.

Culinary Preparations: The Osage Orange is not typically used for culinary purposes due to its inedible fruit. However, the wood is highly valued for its durability and is used for fence posts, furniture, and woodworking projects.

Medicinal Uses: The Osage Orange has had some traditional medicinal uses, including treating skin conditions and as an anti-inflammatory. However, modern scientific evidence supporting these claims is limited.

Fun or Historical Fact: The Osage Orange played a role in American history. The thorny branches were planted by settlers as natural fences to contain livestock before the invention of barbed wire.

Dog Toxicity: The fruit of the Osage Orange is not considered toxic to dogs, but consumption can cause gastrointestinal upset, including vomiting and diarrhea.

Southern Magnolia

Magnolia grandiflora [MAG-NO-LEE-UH GRAN-DIH-FLOR-UH]

Southern Magnolia is a stunning evergreen tree belonging to the Magnoliaceae family. Known for its large, fragrant flowers and glossy, dark green leaves, Southern Magnolia symbolizes the South and has a long history of use in landscaping and as an ornamental tree. Other common names for Southern Magnolia include Bull Bay and Evergreen Magnolia. The tree's wood has been used for furniture, veneer, and cabinetry, while the leaves and flowers have been used in traditional medicine.

Location: Native to the southeastern United States, Southern Magnolia is found in East Texas, where it grows in moist, well-drained soils. It's often seen as an ornamental tree in woodlands, streams, rivers, and residential areas.

Identification:

G‌ROWTH/S‌IZE: A medium to large-sized tree, reaching heights of 60 to 80 feet and sometimes up to 100 feet under favorable conditions. It has a pyramidal or rounded crown with a spread of 30 to 50 feet.

B‌ARK/S‌TEM/R‌OOT: The bark is thin, smooth, and gray when young, becoming darker and scaly with age. The tree's branches are stout and horizontally spreading, supporting its large leaves and flowers.

L‌EAF: The evergreen leaves are simple, alternate, and leathery. They measure 5 to 8 inches long and 2 to 4 inches wide, with a glossy dark green upper surface and a brown, rusty, or silvery underside.

F‌LOWER: It's famous for its large, showy, and fragrant flowers. The white, cup-shaped flowers can be 8 to 12 inches in diameter and usually bloom from late spring to early summer. The flowers have a pleasant, lemony scent.

F‌RUIT/S‌EED/N‌UT: After flowering, it produces a cone-like fruiting structure called an aggregate of follicles. The fruit is 2 to 4 inches long and matures from green to reddish-brown. It contains bright red seeds that are eventually released as the fruit dries and splits open.

Look-A-Like Plant(s): Southern Magnolia may be confused with other Magnolia species like **Sweetbay Magnolia** (*Magnolia virginiana*) or **Bigleaf Magnolia** (*Magnolia macrophylla*). However, the size and fragrance of the flowers, along with the tree's evergreen nature, help differentiate Southern Magnolia from its relatives.

Cautions: There are no significant cautions associated with Southern Magnolia. However, the tree can drop leaves and fruit, which may create a mess in some landscapes.

Culinary Preparations: Southern Magnolia is not commonly used for culinary purposes.

Medicinal Uses: Traditionally, Native Americans and early settlers used various parts of Southern Magnolia for medicinal purposes. A tea made from the bark was used to treat fevers, rheumatism, and stomach problems, while the leaves were used to treat toothaches, and the flowers were believed to have a calming effect.

Fun or Historical Fact: Southern Magnolia has been a famous ornamental tree in the South since the 18th century when it was introduced to Europe as an exotic species. Its large, fragrant flowers and evergreen foliage have made it a symbol of Southern grace and hospitality.

Dog Toxicity: Southern Magnolia is not considered toxic to dogs.

PART SEVEN
MAGICAL MYCOLOGY
UNEARTHING THE FASCINATING WORLD OF TEXAS MUSHROOMS AND FUNGI

Mushroom foraging can be fun and rewarding. Still, it is crucial to be cautious and correctly identify mushrooms before consuming them. Many wild mushrooms are poisonous and can cause severe illness or even death if ingested.

Learning how to correctly identify mushrooms by consulting field guides, attending foraging classes, or going out with experienced foragers is essential. Some key characteristics to look for include the cap, stem, and gills' shape, color, and texture. It's also important to take note of the mushroom's habitat and the plants and trees it is growing near.

When foraging, avoid mushrooms with white gills; they are often toxic. Also, it's necessary to avoid mushrooms with red color on the cap or stem since many poisonous mushrooms have red pigmentation.

It's also important to never eat raw mushrooms because some toxic mushrooms can cause severe reactions.

It's also important to note that some mushrooms may be edible but cause allergic reactions in specific individuals. Hence, it is vital to start with small portions when trying a new mushroom species.

It is always best to err on the side of caution and only consume mushrooms that an expert has positively identified.

CHAPTER 58
SAFEST WAY TO COOK MUSHROOMS
UNLOCKING FLAVOR AND NUTRITION

Cooking mushrooms enhance their taste and helps break down their cell walls, making nutrients more accessible and reducing potentially harmful compounds. To ensure you're cooking mushrooms safely and deliciously, follow these tactics, temps, and cooking methods.

1. **Clean mushrooms gently:** Use a damp paper towel or a soft brush to remove dirt and debris. Avoid soaking them in water, as they can become waterlogged and lose their texture.
2. **Choose the proper cooking method:** There are various ways to cook mushrooms, including sautéing, roasting, grilling, and stir-frying. Sautéing is a popular method that involves cooking mushrooms in a bit of oil or butter over medium heat, which helps to release their natural moisture and develop a rich flavor. Roasting and grilling mushrooms at a high temperature can create a crispy, golden exterior with a tender interior. Stir-frying is another quick and easy way to cook mushrooms while retaining their texture.
3. **Cook at a safe temperature:** To eliminate potentially harmful compounds, cook mushrooms at a minimum temperature of 165°F (74°C). Use a food thermometer to ensure they reach this internal temperature.
4. **Cook until tender and golden:** The ideal texture for cooked mushrooms is tender and slightly golden. This usually takes around 8-10 minutes for sautéing, 15-20 minutes for roasting, and 5-7 minutes for stir-frying. Cooking times may vary depending on the type and size of the mushrooms.

5. **Season to taste:** Enhance the flavor of your mushrooms by seasoning them with salt, pepper, garlic, onions, or your favorite herbs and spices. Add seasonings towards the end of the cooking process to prevent them from burning.

Following these guidelines, you can safely cook mushrooms to unlock their full flavor potential and nutritional benefits while reducing any risks of consuming them raw.

A rtist's Conk

Ganoderma applanatum [GUH-NOH-DUR-MUH AP-PLUH-NAY-TUHM]

Artist's Conk is a fascinating fungus that belongs to the Ganodermataceae family. This bracket fungus is known for its woody texture and the ability to create intricate designs on its surface. Other common names for Artist's Conk include Artist's Bracket and Bear Bread. It has traditionally been used for creating natural artworks and medicinal purposes.

Location: While not native to Texas, Artist's Conk can be found throughout the United States, including Texas. It grows on a variety of hardwood trees, particularly on dead or dying trees or fallen logs. It prefers shady, damp, and wooded environments.

Identification:

CAP: The cap is large, flat, and semicircular or kidney-shaped. It can range from 2 to 24 inches across and up to 8 inches thick. The upper surface is rough, with a brown to grayish-brown color and a white margin.

Hymenium: The hymenium (fertile, spore-producing surface) is white and porous, with tiny pores that release spores. When touched or scratched, the surface bruises, leaving a dark brown mark, which is why it's used for creating art.

Stipe: Artist's Conk typically lacks a stipe or has a rudimentary, poorly developed one.

Spore Print: The spore print is brown.

Ecology: As a saprobic fungus, it decomposes dead or dying wood, which is essential to nutrient recycling within ecosystems.

Look-A-Like Mushroom(s): Ganoderma lucidum, also known as Lingzhi or Reishi, is similar in appearance to Artist's Conk. However, it has a shiny, reddish cap and a more well-defined stipe.

Cautions: Artist's Conk is not poisonous, but its tough, woody texture makes it inedible. Be cautious when handling the fungus, as the spores may cause respiratory irritation in sensitive individuals.

Culinary Preparations: Artist's Conk is not used in culinary preparations due to its inedible, woody nature.

Medicinal Uses: Artist's Conk has historically been used in traditional Chinese medicine for its immune-boosting and anti-inflammatory properties. Modern research suggests it may contain bioactive compounds with potential anticancer, antioxidant, and antiviral effects.

Fun or Historical Fact: The unique bruising property of Artist's Conk has made it a popular medium for creating intricate, long-lasting art pieces. Artists can draw on the white surface, and the etched designs turn dark brown, creating beautiful, natural artwork.

Devil's Cigar

Chorioactis Geaster [KOR-EE-OH-AK-TIS JEE-STER]

So this one is just a bonus as it is not edible and has no medicinal value. I'm only including it in this guide because it's the official state mushroom of Texas. The Devil's Cigar is a rare and intriguing fungus from the Chorioactidaceae family. This fascinating fungus is also known as the Texas Star or Devil's Horn, owing to its unusual appearance. Devil's Cigar has not been documented for any specific traditional uses, but its distinctive appearance has long piqued the curiosity of nature enthusiasts and mycologists.

Location: Devil's Cigar is native to Texas and parts of Japan, making it an exceptionally rare and geographically restricted fungus. In Texas, it can be found in the central and eastern parts of the state, where it grows on decaying hardwood stumps and roots.

Identification:

Cap: It has a unique cap that resembles a dark brown cigar or horn-like structure. It measures about 2 to 4 inches in length, and when it "blooms," it opens up to reveal a star-shaped arrangement of 4 to 7 rays.

Hymenium: The hymenium is smooth and lies on the inner surfaces of the rays when the cap opens up.

Stipe: It lacks a typical stipe or stem, as it emerges directly from decaying wood.

Spore Print: The spore print is white. To obtain a spore print, place the open star-shaped cap, hymenium-side down, on a sheet of paper or foil for several hours or overnight.

Ecology: Devil's Cigar is a saprobic fungus that feeds on decaying organic matter. It helps break down hardwood stumps and roots, contributing to the decomposition and recycling of nutrients in forest ecosystems.

Look-A-Like Plants: There are no known toxic look-alikes for Devil's Cigar. Its unique appearance, with its cigar-like structure that opens into a star shape, sets it apart from other fungi.

Cautions: While Devil's Cigar is not known to be toxic, it is a rare and ecologically significant fungus. Collecting it may be discouraged to help preserve its population in the wild.

Culinary Preparations: Devil's Cigar is not known to be edible and has no documented culinary uses.

Medicinal Uses: There are no known traditional or modern medicinal uses for Devil's Cigar.

Fun or Historical Fact: One of the most fascinating aspects of Devil's Cigar is its method of spore dispersal. When the fungus "blooms" and opens into its star shape, it releases a cloud of spores with an audible hissing sound, earning it the nickname "Devil's Cigar." This unique spore dispersal mechanism adds to the allure and mystique of this already captivating fungus.

D ryad's Saddle

Polyporus squamosus [POH-LIH-PAWR-UHS SKWUH-MOH-SUHSS]

Dryad's Saddle is a type of bracket fungus that belongs to the Polyporaceae family. This distinctive fungus is known by several other names, including Pheasant's Back Mushroom and Hawk's Wing. The original use of Dryad's Saddle was primarily culinary, as it has been harvested for centuries as a wild edible mushroom.

Location: Dryad's Saddle is native to North America, Europe, and Asia. Although it is not specifically native to Texas, it can be found throughout most of the United States, including the eastern, central, and southern regions. This mushroom typically grows on dead or dying hardwood trees like elm, ash, or maple.

Identification:

CAP: The cap of Dryad's Saddle measures between 4 to 12 inches in diameter. It is fan-shaped or semicircular, with a light to dark brown background covered in darker brown scales. The cap is slightly wavy and often develops irregular lobes.

Hʏᴍᴇɴɪᴜᴍ: The hymenium is composed of small pores on the cap's underside. These pores are initially white but become yellowish as the mushroom ages. They are approximately 1/16 to 1/8 inch in diameter.

Sᴛɪᴘᴇ: It has a short, thick stipe measuring about 1 to 3 inches long. It is centrally attached to the cap and often partially or entirely hidden.

Sᴘᴏʀᴇ Pʀɪɴᴛ: The spore print is white, making identifying this mushroom among other bracket fungi easier.

Eᴄᴏʟᴏɢʏ: Dryad's Saddle is a saprotrophic fungus that decomposes dead or dying wood, particularly hardwoods. The mushroom usually appears in the spring and early summer, growing singly or in overlapping clusters on tree trunks and stumps.

Look-A-Like Mushroom(s): There are no significantly toxic look-alikes to Dryad's Saddle, but it can sometimes be confused with other Polyporus species, which are generally considered inedible due to their tough texture.

Cautions: While Dryad's Saddle is considered edible, it's essential to correctly identify it before consuming it. Only harvest young and tender specimens, as older ones can become tough and inedible.

Culinary Preparations: Young and tender Dryad's Saddle mushrooms can be used in various culinary preparations. They can be sliced and sautéed in butter or oil, added to soups, stews, stir-fries, or even pickled for long-term storage. The mushroom has a mild, nutty flavor with a slight cucumber-like aroma.

Medicinal Uses: While Dryad's Saddle has no widely recognized medicinal uses, it has been used in traditional medicine in some cultures for its purported anti-inflammatory and antimicrobial properties.

Fun or Historical Fact: The name "Dryad's Saddle" is inspired by the mythological dryads, tree-dwelling nymphs in Greek mythology. The name suggests that these nymphs might use the mushroom as a saddle when riding through the forest.

E noki

Flammulina velutipes [FLAM-YOO-LEE-NUH VUH-LOO-TUH-PEEZ]

Enoki mushrooms belong to the Physalacriaceae family. This unique mushroom is characterized by its long, slender stems and tiny white caps. It's known by other names such as Golden Needle, Lily, Velvet Foot, and Winter Mushroom. Enoki has been cultivated and consumed in Asia for centuries, particularly in Japan, China, and Korea.

Location: Enoki is native to East Asia and is commonly found in countries like Japan, China, and Korea. It is not native to Texas or the United States. However, these mushrooms can be cultivated indoors or outdoors and grown and consumed worldwide.

Identification:

CAP: The caps are small, round, and white to cream-colored, typically measuring 0.2 to 0.8 inches in diameter. The caps are smooth and have a slightly slimy texture when wet.

Hymenium: The hymenium (the fertile, spore-bearing surface) consists of gills, which are white and closely spaced.

Stipe: The stipe is long, slender, and white to pale yellow, measuring 2 to 5 inches long and 0.1 to 0.2 inches in diameter. The base of the stipe is covered in dark brown, velvety hairs, which is why the mushroom is sometimes called Velvet Foot.

Spore Print: The spore prints are white.

Ecology: They are saprotrophic, meaning they feed on decaying organic matter. They typically grow on the deadwood of broadleaf trees like elm, ash, and mulberry. Enoki mushrooms are cold-weather mushrooms and usually fruit from late autumn to early winter.

Look-A-Like Mushroom(s): They may resemble other long-stemmed, small-capped mushrooms like the **Fairy Inkcap** (*Coprinellus disseminatus*) or the **Slender Stipe** (*Oudemansiella longipes*). However, these look-alikes are not toxic and are considered edible, though they may not have the same culinary appeal as Enoki.

Cautions: They are generally safe to consume. However, purchasing them from a reputable source or cultivating them properly is essential.

Culinary Preparations: They are popular in Asian cuisine, particularly soups, stir-fries, and salads. Their mild, slightly sweet flavor and crunchy texture make them versatile ingredients. They can be eaten raw, but cooking them enhances their flavor. To prepare them, trim off the base, separate the stems, and rinse them gently.

Medicinal Uses: Traditionally, they have been used in Asian medicine for their immune-boosting and anticancer properties. Modern studies have shown that they contain compounds like beta-glucans and flammulin, which may have potential health benefits, including supporting the immune system and possessing anti-tumor properties.

Fun or Historical Fact: They were initially cultivated in Japan over 1,000 years ago. They were grown in the dark to maintain their pale color and elongate their stems. Today, they are widely cultivated using similar techniques in temperature and light-controlled environments to produce the characteristic long stems and small caps.

I ndigo Milkcap

Lactarius indigo [Lack-TARE-ee-us IN-dih-goh]

The Indigo Milkcap is a unique, eye-catching mushroom belonging to the Russulaceae family. This fascinating fungus is known for its vibrant blue color and the blue "milk" or latex it exudes when damaged. Other common names for the Indigo Milkcap include Blue Milk Mushroom and Blue Lactarius.

Location: It's native to North America and predominantly found in the southern and eastern United States, including Texas. It is commonly found in mixed woodlands near pine and oak trees. The mushrooms typically appear during the summer and fall months.

Identification:

Cap: The cap is convex, becoming flat or slightly depressed with age. It measures 2 to 6 inches in diameter and is a vibrant blue color, with the shade often becoming paler as the mushroom ages. The surface of the cap is smooth and slightly sticky when wet.

Hymenium: The hymenium, or the spore-producing surface, consists of closely spaced gills that exhibit the same bright blue color as the cap. When damaged, the gills exude a blue "milk" or latex, a key identifying feature of this mushroom.

Stipe: The stipe is cylindrical and measures 1 to 4 inches long and 0.5 to 1 inch in diameter. The stipe is also blue and slightly lighter or darker than the cap.

Spore Print: The spore print is pale cream to buff in color.

Ecology: This mycorrhizal mushroom forms a symbiotic relationship with the roots of various tree species, particularly pines and oaks. It plays an essential role in the nutrient exchange between the fungus and the host tree.

Look-A-Like Mushroom(s): While the Indigo Milkcap is quite distinct in appearance, there are a few similar species. The **Silent-colored milkcap** (*Lactarius quieticolor*) and the **Yellow latex milky cap (***Lactarius chelidonium***)** are two examples. Still, they lack the vibrant blue color and blue latex of the Indigo Milkcap.

Cautions: The Indigo Milkcap is generally considered edible.

Culinary Preparations: The Indigo Milkcap is edible and has a mild, slightly sweet, and nutty flavor. It can be sautéed, fried, or added to soups and stews. The blue color may fade when cooked, but the taste remains delicious.

Medicinal Uses: While there are no well-documented medicinal uses for the Indigo Milkcap, it has been used by some traditional healers for its presumed anti-inflammatory and antioxidant properties.

A Fun Fact: The vibrant blue color of the Indigo Milkcap is quite rare among mushrooms, making it an exciting find for mushroom enthusiasts and foragers. It is one of the few naturally blue-colored mushrooms found in the wild.

Grey Knight

Tricholoma equestre [TRIH-KOL-uh-muh ee-KWES-tree]

Grey Knight is a member of the Tricholomataceae family. Other common names for Grey Knight include "Dirty Trich" and "Earth Fan." The original use of this mushroom was for culinary purposes, as it is considered an edible species.

Location: It's are native to many parts of the world, including North America and Europe. They are not specifically native to Texas but can be found there. Grey Knight mushrooms grow in forests, often under conifers and hardwood trees.

Identification:

GROWTH/SIZE: It usually grows to 2 to 4 inches.

CAP: The cap is typically 1.5 to 4 inches wide. It is grey or grey-brown, with a convex shape that flattens out as it matures.

Hymenium: The hymenium, or the spore-bearing surface of the mushroom, consists of grey or grey-brown gills connected to the stipe (stem).

Stipe: The stipe is 1.5 to 4 inches long and usually has a thickness of about 0.5 inches. It is often the same color as the cap and may be slightly thicker at the base.

Spore Print: It has a white spore print.

Ecology: These mushrooms grow in the soil, usually in the fall, and are commonly found in forests, especially under conifer and hardwood trees.

Look-A-Like Plants: It can look similar to other grey or brown-capped mushrooms. Some toxic look-a-likes include the poisonous **Tigertop** (*Tricholoma pardinum*), which has a more scaly cap and darker gills.

Cautions: Always be cautious when foraging mushrooms, as misidentification can lead to serious health problems. If you are unsure about identifying a mushroom, consult an expert before consuming it.

Culinary Preparations: It can be eaten when cooked. They can be added to soups, stews or sautéed in butter or oil. Always cook them thoroughly, as eating raw mushrooms may cause digestive issues.

Medicinal Uses: There are no well-known medicinal uses for Grey Knight mushrooms. They are primarily used for culinary purposes.

A Fun or Historical Fact: Grey Knight mushrooms have been enjoyed as a food source for centuries. Their unique flavor and texture make them a favorite among mushroom enthusiasts, and their widespread distribution makes them accessible to many worldwide.

S hort-Stemmed Russula

Russula brevipes [RUH-SOO-LUH BREV-IH-PEEZ]

The Short-Stemmed Russula is a fascinating mushroom belonging to the Russulaceae family. This fungi, also known as the White Russula or Short-stemmed White Russula, doesn't have a long history of use. Still, it's well-known among mushroom enthusiasts for its unique appearance and characteristics.

Location: The Short-Stemmed Russula is native to North America, including Texas. It can be found in the state's eastern, southern, and central parts. The mushroom grows in deciduous and mixed forests, forming mycorrhizal relationships with tree species, such as oaks and pines.

Identification:

CAP: The cap measures 2 to 5 inches across and is white to cream-colored. It has a convex shape when young, becoming more flattened and even slightly depressed as it ages. The cap's surface is smooth and sometimes somewhat sticky when wet.

HYMENIUM: The hymenium consists of white to cream-colored gills crowded together and attached to the stipe. The gills are brittle and can break easily when handled.

STIPE: It has a stout and short stipe that measures 1 to 2 inches long and 0.6 to 1.5 inches thick. The stipe is white and sometimes has a slightly swollen base. Its surface is smooth, sometimes with faint vertical grooves.

SPORE PRINT: The spore print is white to cream-colored, helping to distinguish it from other species.

ECOLOGY: The Short-Stemmed Russula is a mycorrhizal fungus that forms symbiotic relationships with trees, particularly oaks and pines. It helps the trees absorb nutrients while receiving carbohydrates in return. The mushroom grows solitary or in small groups from late summer to fall.

Look-A-Like Mushroom(s): The Short-Stemmed Russula can be confused with other white-capped Russula species, such as Russula delica or Russula albonigra. It's essential to carefully examine the mushroom's characteristics and habitat to ensure accurate identification.

Cautions: While the Short-Stemmed Russula is edible, some people may experience gastrointestinal upset after consuming it. It's essential to cook the mushroom thoroughly before eating and to try a small amount first to ensure no adverse reactions.

Culinary Preparations: Short-Stemmed Russula can be used in a variety of dishes. It can be sautéed, added to soups or stews, or used as a pizza topping. The mushroom has a mild, nutty flavor and a firm texture.

Medicinal Uses: There are no known traditional or modern medicinal uses for the Short-Stemmed Russula.

Fun or Historical Fact: The Short-Stemmed Russula is sometimes used as a "host" for the parasitic fungus, Hypomyces lactifluorum, transforming it into the highly prized and delicious Lobster Mushroom. The parasitic fungus engulfs the mushroom, turning it bright orange and giving it a seafood-like aroma and flavor.

S now Fungus

Tremella fuciformis [TRUH-MEL-UH FYOO-KUH-FORM-ISS]

Snow Fungus is a type of edible fungus belonging to the Tremellaceae family. Known for its gelatinous texture and mild taste, it has been used in traditional Chinese cuisine and medicine for centuries. Other common names for Snow Fungus include White Jelly Mushroom, Silver Ear Fungus, and White Wood Ear.

Location: Snow Fungus is native to the tropics and subtropics of Asia, including China, Japan, and Southeast Asia. However, it has been introduced to other parts of the world, including North America. In Texas, it can grow on dead or decaying hardwood branches, particularly during the warmer and wetter months.

Identification:

CAP: Snow Fungus has a translucent, white, or pale yellow cap that is gelatinous and lobed. The cap can measure 1 to 4 inches across and has an irregular, brain-like appearance.

Hymenium: The hymenium, or fertile spore-producing surface, is spread across the entire cap. The smooth, jelly-like surface lacks the gills or pores typical of many mushrooms.

Stipe: It does not have a distinct stipe or stem. Instead, it attaches directly to the substrate by a small, inconspicuous base.

Spore Print: The spore print is white, which can be difficult to see on a white background. Place the cap on a dark surface to collect the spore print.

Ecology: Snow Fungus is a saprobic fungus that decomposes dead organic matter. It is commonly found on decaying hardwood branches in tropical and subtropical regions.

Look-A-Like Mushroom(s): There are a few look-a-like fungi, including the **Hairy White Jelly Fungus** (*Exidia thuretiana*) and the **White Brain Fungus** (*Exidia nucleata*). These species are also gelatinous but generally smaller and have different textures.

Cautions: none known.

Culinary Preparations: Snow Fungus is used in various Asian dishes, including sweet and savory soups and desserts. It is often soaked and rehydrated before cooking, as it has a crunchy, gelatinous texture. Everyday recipes include sweet snow fungus soup with goji berries or savory dishes with vegetables and meats.

Medicinal Uses: Traditional Chinese medicine has long recognized Snow Fungus for its health benefits. It is believed to boost the immune system, improve respiratory health, and promote skin elasticity. Modern research has found potential anti-inflammatory, antioxidant, and neuroprotective properties in Snow Fungus.

Fun or Historical Fact: Snow Fungus has been a delicacy in Chinese cuisine for over 2,000 years. It was once considered a rare and valuable ingredient, reserved only for the Chinese Imperial Court. Today, it is enjoyed by people worldwide for its unique texture and health benefits.

S traw Mushroom

Volvariella volvacea [VAHL-VUH-REE-EL-UH VAHL-VUH-SEE-UH]

The Straw Mushroom is a popular edible mushroom belonging to the Pluteaceae family. Known for its delicious taste and meaty texture, this mushroom is commonly used in Asian cuisine. Other common names for Straw Mushrooms include Paddy Straw Mushroom and Chinese Mushroom. It has been cultivated and consumed for centuries, particularly in China and Southeast Asia.

Location: Though not native to Texas, Straw Mushrooms can be cultivated in the state under controlled conditions. They are typically grown on rice straw beds, which provide an ideal environment for their growth.

Identification:

CAP: The cap measures 1.5 to 4 inches in diameter. It starts as an egg-shaped structure and later opens up, revealing a convex or flat surface. The color varies from pale grayish-brown to dark brown, sometimes with a slightly metallic sheen.

Hymenium: The hymenium, or spore-producing surface, is pinkish in young Straw Mushrooms, turning dark brown as they mature. It features closely spaced gills that are free from the stipe.

Stipe: The stipe is 2 to 5 inches long and 0.4 to 0.8 inches thick. It is white, smooth, and cylindrical, often tapering toward the base. The base of the stipe is enclosed in a white, membranous, sack-like structure called the volva.

Spore Print: The spore print is salmon pink to dark brown, which can be obtained by placing the cap gill-side down on a piece of paper or foil.

Ecology: Straw Mushrooms are saprobic, meaning they decompose dead organic matter. They thrive in warm, humid environments and are commonly found growing on decomposing rice straws, hence their name.

Look-A-Like Mushroom(s): Straw Mushrooms can be confused with the toxic Amanita mushrooms, specifically, the **Death Cap** (*Amanita phalloides*) and **Destroying Angel** (*Amanita virosa*), which also have a volva at the base of their stipe. Proper identification is crucial to avoid accidental consumption of toxic mushrooms.

Cautions: Always ensure accurate identification before consuming Straw Mushrooms, as they can be easily confused with toxic Amanita species. Consuming toxic mushrooms can lead to severe poisoning or even death.

Culinary Preparations: Straw Mushrooms are a popular ingredient in various Asian dishes, such as stir-fries, soups, and curries. They can be eaten fresh or dried and rehydrated before cooking. Their meaty texture and savory flavor make them a delicious addition to a variety of recipes.

Medicinal Uses: While Straw Mushrooms are mainly consumed for their taste, they also contain essential nutrients and antioxidants, which can help boost the immune system and support overall health.

Fun or Historical Fact: Straw Mushrooms are one of the fastest-growing mushrooms globally, with some strains that can double in size within just 24 hours under optimal growing conditions. This rapid growth rate has made them a popular choice for commercial cultivation.

Western Giant Puffball

Calvatia booniana [KAL-VAY-SHUH BOO-NEE-AY-NUH]

The Western Giant Puffball is a fascinating and unusual fungus from the Agaricaceae family. Also known as the Earthball or Star Earthball, this puffball has captivated the interest of both amateur and professional mycologists for years.

Location: Native to the southwestern United States, including Texas, the Puffball prefers to grow in arid and semi-arid environments. It is often found in the central and western parts of Texas, thriving in sandy soils, desert scrublands, and grasslands.

Identification:

CAP: It has a round to slightly flattened cap that measures between 1 and 2 inches in diameter. The outer surface of the cap is covered in small, conical warts or spikes, which give the puffball its unique star-like appearance.

Hymenium: The hymenium, or spore-producing surface, is hidden within the cap. As the puffball matures, the outer layer of the cap will rupture, releasing a cloud of spores.

Stipe: This puffball lacks a distinct stipe or stalk. It is sessile, meaning it grows directly on the ground or substrate.

Spore Print: The spore print is brown to dark brown.

Ecology: The Puffball is a saprophytic fungus, which means it decomposes organic matter in the soil. It helps break down dead plant material and recycle nutrients back into the ecosystem.

Look-A-Like Mushroom(s): The Puffball can be confused with other puffball species, such as the Common Puffball (Lycoperdon perlatum) and the Giant Puffball (Calvatia gigantea). However, the unique star-like appearance of the Texas Star Puffball sets it apart from other puffballs.

Cautions: When collecting any wild mushrooms, it is essential to exercise caution and positively identify the species. Consuming toxic mushrooms can lead to severe illness or even death. It is always recommended to consult a local expert or field guide when in doubt.

Culinary Preparations: The Western Giant Puffball is considered edible when young and firm, with a solid white interior. It can be sliced and sautéed in butter or oil, added to stir-fries, or used as a substitute for other puffball species in recipes.

Medicinal Uses: There are no known medicinal uses for the Texas Star Puffball.

Fun or Historical Fact: The Western Giant Puffball gets its name from the distinctive star-like pattern created by conical warts on its cap, which resembles the iconic "Lone Star" symbol of Texas.

Wine Cap

Stropharia rugosoannulata [stroh-FAIR-ee-uh roo-goh-soh-AN-yoo-LAH-tuh]

Wine Cap is a popular edible mushroom belonging to the Strophariaceae family. It is also commonly referred to as the King Stropharia, Garden Giant, or Burgundy Mushroom due to its large size and distinctive color. Wine Cap mushrooms have been appreciated for their delicious taste and nutritional value since ancient times.

Location: It's native to North America and Europe but has been introduced to various parts of the world. Although not specifically native to Texas, it can be found throughout the state, especially in gardens, wood chips, and mulched areas. It thrives in rich, moist, and well-draining soils, making it an excellent candidate for cultivation in home gardens.

Identification:

CAP: The cap ranges from 2 to 12 inches in diameter, with a convex to a flat shape. The cap's color can vary from deep wine-red to tan, often fading with age or in sunlight.

HYMENIUM: It features closely spaced gills that are initially pale and turn purplish-brown as the mushroom matures. The gills are attached to the stipe and sometimes run slightly down its length.

STIPE: The stipe is sturdy and measures 3 to 8 inches long and about 0.5 to 1.5 inches thick. The stipe is often white, sometimes with reddish tones, and has a distinctive thick, white, and membranous ring.

SPORE PRINT: The spore print is dark purple-brown, which can help identify the mushroom.

ECOLOGY: Wine Cap is a saprotrophic fungus that decomposes organic matter, primarily wood chips and other woody debris. It plays a vital role in breaking down and recycling nutrients in its environment.

Look-A-Like Mushroom(s): The Wine Cap mushroom can be confused with some toxic species, such as the **Deadly Galerina** (*Galerina marginata*). However, the spore print of Deadly Galerina is rusty brown, differentiating it from the dark purple-brown spore print of the Wine Cap. Always exercise caution and consult an expert if you're unsure about mushroom identification.

Cautions: While Wine Cap is an edible and delicious mushroom, it's essential to be cautious when foraging. Misidentifying mushrooms can lead to severe poisoning or even death. Only consume mushrooms you're confident about; consult an expert if you're uncertain.

Culinary Preparations: Wine Cap mushrooms are highly versatile in cooking and can be used in various dishes, such as sautés, stir-fries, soups, and stews. Their meaty texture and rich flavor make them an excellent addition to vegetarian and vegan dishes as a meat substitute.

Medicinal Uses: Despite the limited scientific evidence, some traditional herbalists claim that Wine Cap mushrooms may have immune-boosting and anti-inflammatory properties. More research is needed to confirm these potential benefits.

Fun Fact: Wine Cap mushrooms are delicious and beneficial to the environment. As decomposers, they help recycle nutrients and improve soil quality, making them an excellent addition to permaculture and sustainable gardening practices.

PART EIGHT

BEWARE THE BANE OF TEXAS

A GUIDE TO POISONOUS PLANTS

Bracken Fern

Pteridium aquilinum [TEH-RID-ee-um AH-KWIL-uh-nuhm]

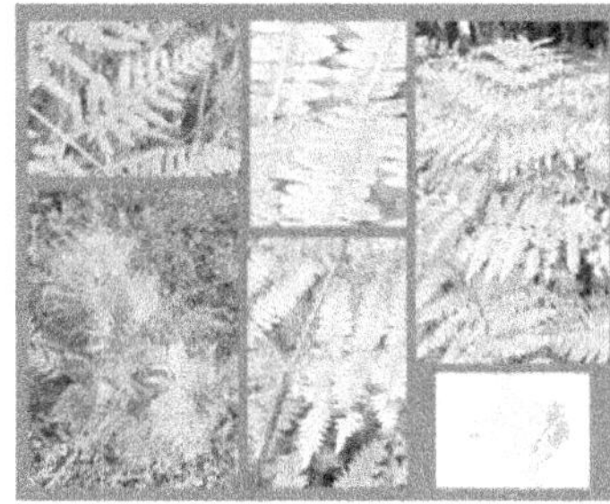

Bracken Fern is a member of the Dennstaedtiaceae family and is also known by other names, like "Eagle Fern" and "Common Bracken." This hardy fern has a long history and can be found in various parts of the world, from North America to Asia. Bracken Ferns have some look-a-like plants that you should be aware of. One of these is the non-toxic **Lady Fern** which has a similar appearance but with more delicate, lacy fronds. Another look-a-like is the toxic **Cinnamon Fern**, which has cinnamon-colored, fertile fronds that set it apart from the Bracken Fern. While Bracken Ferns contain carcinogenic compounds, meaning they can cause cancer if consumed in large amounts over a long period. So, while the Bracken Fern is a fascinating plant with a long history, it's essential to remember its potential dangers. Always be cautious when handling or foraging for plants, especially if you have animals that might be tempted to snack on them.

Oleander

Nerium oleander [NUH-REE-UHM OH-LEE-AN-DER]

Belongs to the dogbane family, Apocynaceae. This eye-catching plant goes by other common names like Rose Laurel and Rosebay. Although Oleander is beautiful, it's essential to be aware of its toxic nature. Some non-toxic plants that look similar to Oleander include the **Rose of Sharon** and the **Crape Myrtle**. These plants are often used as alternatives in gardens because they're safe and still provide stunning blooms. It's crucial to be cautious around Oleander, as every part of this plant is poisonous, containing compounds called cardiac glycosides. If ingested, even in small amounts, it can lead to severe symptoms and even death in humans and animals. Signs of Oleander poisoning include nausea, vomiting, stomach pain, diarrhea, dizziness, weakness, and irregular heartbeat. More severe symptoms involve difficulty breathing, seizures, and even coma.

Texas Mountain Laurel

Sophora secundiflora [SUH-FOHR-UH SEK-UHN-DIH-FLOR-UH]

Texas Mountain Laurel belongs to the Fabaceae plant family. Several other names, such as Mescal Bean and Frijolito, are a few. With its stunning purple flowers, it's no wonder this native Texan shrub has a history of adorning landscapes and gardens. One look-a-like is the non-toxic **Eve's Necklace**, which has pink flowers instead of purple. Another look-a-like is the toxic **Carolina jessamine**, which has yellow, trumpet-shaped flowers. Make sure to correctly identify Texas Mountain Laurel before handling or planting it in your garden. The plant produces red, bean-like seeds that are highly toxic if ingested. If you have children or pets, keeping them away from the seeds is vital. Ingesting the seeds can cause symptoms like dizziness, vomiting, and, in severe cases, even death. If you suspect that someone has consumed the seeds, seek medical attention immediately.

Chinaberry

Melia azedarach [MEE-LEE-UH AH-ZUH-DUH-RAK]

Chinaberry is a fascinating tree that belongs to the Meliaceae family. It has several other common names, such as Persian Lilac, Pride of India, and Bead Tree. It has a few look-a-like plants, both toxic and non-toxic. A non-toxic look-a-like is the **Crape Myrtle**, which has similar-looking flowers and leaves but lacks the distinctive yellow berries of the Chinaberry tree. On the other hand, a toxic look-a-like is **Heavenly Bamboo** which has similar-looking berries but a different leaf structure. It's essential to be cautious around Chinaberry trees, as they have toxic properties. All parts of the tree, especially the berries, are toxic to humans and animals if ingested. Symptoms of Chinaberry poisoning can include vomiting, diarrhea, weakness, seizures, and even respiratory failure in severe cases.

Castor Bean

Ricinus communis [RI-SY-NUHS KUH-MYOO-NIS]

The Castor Bean is a member of the Euphorbiaceae family. Other common names for the Castor Bean plant include "Palma Christi" and "Wonder Tree." It's important to remember that the Castor Bean plant itself is highly toxic. The seeds contain a deadly toxin called ricin, which can be lethal if ingested. If someone accidentally ingests Castor Bean seeds, they may experience symptoms like nausea, vomiting, abdominal pain, diarrhea, and dehydration. It can lead to seizures, organ failure, and even death in severe cases. It has been used for centuries in various cultures for its beneficial properties. Castor oil, which is extracted from seeds, has been used as a natural remedy for various ailments and is still a popular ingredient in cosmetics and skin care products today.

Yellow Jessamine

Gelsemium sempervirens [JEL-SEE-MEE-UM SEM-PER-VYE-RENZ]

Yellow Jessamine belongs to the Gelsemiaceae family and is known by other common names like Carolina Jessamine, Evening Trumpetflower, and Woodbine. This climbing vine is famous for its bright yellow, trumpet-shaped flowers that bloom in late winter or early spring, adding a splash of color to the landscape. While Yellow Jessamine is quite distinctive, it may be confused with other plants like **Honeysuckle** and **Trumpet Vine**. Both of these plants have trumpet-shaped flowers, but Honeysuckle typically has white, pink, or red flowers, and Trumpet Vine has bright orange or red flowers. Neither of these look-a-likes is toxic. All parts of the Yellow Jessamine, including its flowers, leaves, and roots, contain toxic alkaloids like gelsemine and gelseminine. If ingested, these toxins can cause a range of symptoms, from mild to severe. Mild symptoms include dizziness, headache, and nausea. In extreme cases, more severe symptoms may involve vomiting, difficulty breathing, muscle weakness, seizures, and even death.

W ild Blue Larkspur

Delphinium carolinianum [DEL-FIN-ee-um kair-oh-lin-ee-AH-num]

Wild Blue Larkspur is a stunning wildflower that belongs to the Ranunculaceae family. Other common names for this plant include "Carolina Larkspur" and "Prairie Larkspur." With its vibrant blue-purple flowers, it can easily catch anyone's eye. Wild Blue Larkspur has delicate, irregularly-shaped blooms. There's also a reason to be cautious. While it may be beautiful, it is also toxic if ingested. The plant contains alkaloids, which can cause a variety of symptoms if consumed. These symptoms may include nausea, vomiting, diarrhea, muscle weakness, and even paralysis.

PART NINE
LONE STAR FLAVORS
RECIPES FOR SAVORING THE WILD EDIBLES OF TEXAS

Flameleaf Sumac Spice Blend

Ingredients:

- 1/2 cup Flameleaf Sumac berries
- 1/4 cup salt
- 1/4 cup sesame seeds

Instructions:

1. Rinse the Flameleaf Sumac berries and remove any stems or debris.
2. Spread the berries out on a baking sheet and dry them in the sun or a low oven (150°F) for several hours until they are dry and brittle.
3. Use a food processor, mortar, and pestle to grind the dried berries into a fine powder.
4. Mix the Sumac powder with the salt and sesame seeds in a small bowl.
5. Store the Flameleaf Sumac spice blend in an airtight container in a cool, dry place for up to six months.

This spice blend can season meats, fish, vegetables, salads, and dips. It's especially delicious sprinkled over grilled or roasted chicken or lamb or mixed with olive oil to make a zesty salad dressing. Enjoy!

Mustang Grape Jelly

Prep Time: 1 hour - Cook Time: 1 hour

Servings: Makes approximately 4 cups of jelly

Ingredients:

- 4 cups of Mustang Grapes
- 4 cups of granulated sugar
- 1 packet of powdered pectin
- 1 tablespoon of lemon juice
- Water

Instructions:

1. Wash the grapes thoroughly and remove any stems or leaves.
2. In a large pot, add enough water to cover the grapes and bring them to a boil. Reduce the heat and simmer for 10 minutes.
3. Mash the grapes to release their juices using a potato masher or a fork. Continue to simmer for an additional 10 minutes.
4. Strain the juice into a clean pot using a fine mesh strainer or cheesecloth. Press on the solids to extract as much juice as possible.
5. Add the sugar, lemon juice, and powdered pectin to the pot with the juice and stir until well combined.
6. Bring the mixture to a rolling boil over high heat, stirring constantly. Boil for one minute, then remove from heat.
7. Skim any foam off the top of the jelly with a spoon.
8. Ladle the hot jelly into clean, sterilized jars and seal them with lids.
9. Process the jars in a boiling water bath for 10 minutes to ensure proper sealing.
10. Allow the jars to cool completely before storing them in a cool, dark place.

Enjoy your homemade Mustang Grape Jelly on toast, biscuits, or even as a glaze for meat dishes!

Sweet Acacia Tea

Prep time: 5 minutes

Serving: 2-3 cups

Ingredients:

- 1/4 cup dried Sweet Acacia flowers
- 3 cups of water
- Honey or sugar to taste (optional)

Instructions:

1. Rinse the Sweet Acacia flowers in cold water and then pat them dry.
2. Place the flowers in a teapot or a pot and pour boiling water over them.
3. Let the tea steep for 5-7 minutes or until the desired strength is achieved.
4. Strain the tea into cups and sweeten it with honey or sugar to taste.
5. Serve and enjoy!

Note: You can also add some lemon juice to this tea for a citrusy twist. If you want to make a bigger batch of tea, adjust the amount of Sweet Acacia flowers and water accordingly.

Broadleaf Cattail Fritters

Prep time: Approximately 20-25 minutes

Servings: 4-6 people

Ingredients:

- 1 cup of Broadleaf Cattail shoots, finely chopped
- 1/2 cup of all-purpose flour
- 1/2 cup of cornmeal
- 1/2 tsp of baking powder
- 1/2 tsp of salt
- 1/4 tsp of black pepper
- 1 egg, beaten
- 1/2 cup of milk
- Oil for frying

Instructions:

1. Rinse and finely chop the Broadleaf Cattail shoots. Set aside.
2. Combine the flour, cornmeal, baking powder, salt, and black pepper in a mixing bowl.
3. In another mixing bowl, whisk together the egg and milk.
4. Add the dry ingredients to the wet ingredients and stir until a thick batter forms.
5. Add the chopped Broadleaf Cattail shoots to the batter and stir to coat evenly.
6. Heat a few inches of oil in a heavy-bottomed skillet over medium heat.
7. Using a tablespoon or small ice cream scoop, drop spoonfuls of the batter into the hot oil.
8. Fry the fritters until golden brown and crispy, about 2-3 minutes per side.
9. Remove the fritters from the skillet with a slotted spoon and place them on a paper towel-lined plate to drain excess oil.
10. Repeat with the remaining batter until all the fritters are cooked.

Serve hot and enjoy as a delicious appetizer or side dish!

Greater Mullein infusion

Prep time: 10 minutes

Servings: 1 cup

Ingredients:

- 1 tablespoon of dried Greater Mullein leaves
- 1 cup of boiling water

Instructions:

1. Add the dried Greater Mullein leaves to a teapot or infuser.
2. Pour the boiling water over the leaves and let steep for 10-15 minutes.
3. Strain the tea and discard the leaves.
4. Enjoy the tea hot, or let it cool down and use it as a compress on sore or inflamed skin.

It can be enjoyed as tea or used topically as a soothing compress.

Greater Mullein Tincture

Preparation Time: 2-4 weeks

Servings: 30-40

Ingredients:

- Dried Greater Mullein Leaves (50 grams)
- 100-proof Vodka (500 ml)

Instructions:

1. Take a clean and sterilized glass jar with a tight-fitting lid.
2. Add the dried Greater Mullein leaves to the jar, making sure that they fill up to one-third of the jar.
3. Pour 100-proof vodka over the leaves, filling the jar to the top.
4. Use a clean spoon or a chopstick to stir the mixture and remove any air pockets.
5. Secure the lid tightly and shake the jar for a few minutes.
6. Label the jar with the date and the name of the herb.
7. Store the jar in a cool, dark place for 2-4 weeks. Shake the jar daily to ensure the mixture is well-combined.
8. After 2-4 weeks, strain the tincture through a cheesecloth or a fine-mesh strainer into a clean glass jar or bottle.
9. Store the tincture in a dark, cool place, away from sunlight and heat.

Serving size: 1-2 ml (30-60 drops)

To use the tincture, mix the desired amount with a little water or juice and take it orally, up to 3 times per day. The tincture can be used for respiratory issues, cough, and other conditions. However, consulting with a healthcare professional before starting any new herbal regimen is always recommended.

I ndian Ricegrass Salad

Prep time: 15 minutes

Servings: 4-6

Ingredients:

- 1 cup uncooked Indian Ricegrass
- 1/2 cup chopped red onion
- 1/2 cup chopped cucumber
- 1/2 cup chopped red bell pepper
- 1/4 cup chopped fresh cilantro
- 1/4 cup fresh lemon juice
- 2 tablespoons olive oil
- 1/2 teaspoon ground cumin
- 1/2 teaspoon salt
- 1/4 teaspoon black pepper

Instructions:

1. Rinse the Indian Ricegrass in cold water and drain well. Cook the Indian Ricegrass according to the package instructions until it's tender and fully cooked. Allow the Indian Ricegrass to cool to room temperature.
2. In a large bowl, mix the cooled Indian Ricegrass, red onion, cucumber, red bell pepper, and cilantro together.
3. Whisk together the lemon juice, olive oil, ground cumin, salt, and black pepper in a small bowl. Pour the dressing over the Indian Ricegrass mixture and toss to coat evenly.
4. Serve the Indian Ricegrass salad immediately or refrigerate for up to 1 day. This salad is a great side dish for grilled meats or as a light lunch on its own.

Enjoy!

Lemon Balm Tincture

Preparation Time: 30 minutes

Servings: Depends on the size of your dropper bottle

Ingredients:

- Dried Lemon Balm leaves
- 80-proof alcohol (vodka or brandy)
- Clean jar with lid
- Cheesecloth
- Amber glass dropper bottle

Instructions:

1. Start by filling your jar with dried Lemon Balm leaves. You can either use whole leaves or chop them finely.
2. Pour enough alcohol into the jar to cover the leaves completely. Use 80-proof alcohol, as it has the ideal alcohol content for tinctures.
3. Seal the jar tightly with its lid and shake it gently to mix the leaves and alcohol.
4. Store the jar in a cool, dark place like a pantry or cupboard.
5. Let the mixture infuse for 4-6 weeks, shaking it gently once a day. The alcohol will extract the beneficial compounds from the Lemon Balm leaves, creating a potent tincture.
6. After 4-6 weeks, strain the tincture through a cheesecloth into a clean bowl or measuring cup. Squeeze the cheesecloth to extract as much liquid as possible.
7. Pour the tincture into an amber glass dropper bottle and label it with the name and date.
8. Store the bottle in a cool, dark place, away from sunlight and heat.

To use the Lemon Balm tincture, place a few drops under your tongue or mix it into a glass of water. You can take it up to three times a day.

Note: If you are pregnant, breastfeeding, or taking any medications, consult with a healthcare professional before using any herbal remedies.

Mexican Oregano Salsa

Prep time: 15 minutes

Servings: 6

Ingredients:

- 1 cup chopped fresh tomatoes
- 1/4 cup chopped onion
- 2 cloves garlic, minced
- 2 tablespoons chopped fresh cilantro
- 1 tablespoon fresh lime juice
- 1 teaspoon dried Mexican oregano
- 1/2 teaspoon salt
- 1/4 teaspoon black pepper
- 1/4 teaspoon ground cumin
- 1/4 teaspoon smoked paprika
- 1 jalapeño pepper, seeded and chopped (optional)

Instructions:

1. Combine the chopped tomatoes, onion, garlic, cilantro, and lime juice in a medium bowl.
2. Add the dried Mexican oregano, salt, black pepper, ground cumin, and smoked paprika to the bowl.
3. If desired, add the chopped jalapeño pepper to the bowl.
4. Mix all of the ingredients together until well combined.
5. Cover the bowl and refrigerate for at least 30 minutes before serving to allow the flavors to meld together.
6. Serve the Mexican Oregano Salsa with tortilla chips, or use it as a topping for tacos or grilled meats.

Enjoy!

Yarrow Tea

Prep time: 5 minutes

Servings: 2

Ingredients:

- 1 tablespoon dried yarrow flowers and leaves
- 2 cups water
- honey or lemon (optional)

Instructions:

1. Bring the water to a boil in a pot or kettle.
2. Add the dried yarrow flowers and leaves to the boiling water.
3. Reduce heat to low and let the mixture simmer for 5-10 minutes.
4. Strain the yarrow tea into a teapot or pitcher.
5. Add honey or lemon to taste, if desired.

Serve hot, and enjoy!

Note: Yarrow tea can also be enjoyed cold by letting it cool and adding ice cubes. It is important to consult a healthcare professional before using yarrow tea as a remedy, as it may interact with certain medications or cause allergic reactions in some individuals.

Yarrow tea is a popular herbal remedy used to treat various health issues such as fever, colds, and flu.

Yarrow Tincture

Preparation time: 10 minutes

Servings: 30-40 servings

Ingredients:

- 1 cup of fresh yarrow leaves and flowers
- 1 pint of 100-proof vodka or grain alcohol

Tools:

- A quart-sized mason jar with a lid
- Cheesecloth or a fine-mesh strainer
- A small funnel
- An amber glass dropper bottle

Directions:

1. Rinse the yarrow leaves and flowers and dry them thoroughly.
2. Chop the yarrow leaves and flowers into small pieces and place them in the mason jar.
3. Pour the vodka or grain alcohol over the yarrow until it is completely covered.
4. Seal the mason jar with the lid and shake it vigorously for a few seconds.
5. Store the jar in a cool, dark place for 4-6 weeks, shaking it daily to ensure that the yarrow is fully infused into the alcohol.
6. After 4-6 weeks, strain the mixture through cheesecloth or a fine-mesh strainer into a clean bowl or jar.
7. Transfer the yarrow tincture into an amber glass dropper bottle using the funnel.
8. Store the bottle in a cool, dark place, and use it as needed.

To use the yarrow tincture, place a few drops under your tongue or mix it with a small amount of water. Start with a small amount and gradually increase as needed.

Note: As with any herbal preparation, it's important to consult with a health-care provider before using yarrow tincture, especially if you're pregnant or nursing, or have a medical condition or are taking any medication.

Blackjack Oak Acorn Grits

Prep time: 45 minutes

Servings: 2-3

Ingredients:

- 1 cup Blackjack Oak acorn meal
- 2 cups water
- 1/2 teaspoon salt
- 1 tablespoon honey
- 2 tablespoons vegetable oil

Instructions:

1. Collect ripe acorns from Blackjack Oak trees.
2. Remove the shells and chop the acorns into small pieces.
3. Spread the chopped acorns on a baking sheet and roast them in the oven at 350°F for 30 minutes or until they are golden brown.
4. Let the roasted acorns cool and grind them into a fine meal using a food processor, mortar, and pestle.
5. Bring 2 cups of water to a boil in a saucepan and add 1/2 teaspoon of salt.
6. Add the Blackjack Oak acorn meal to the boiling water and stir constantly for 5-10 minutes or until the mixture becomes thick and creamy.
7. Remove the saucepan from the heat and add 1 tablespoon of honey and 2 tablespoons of vegetable oil.
8. Stir the mixture until everything is well combined, and the honey has melted.
9. Serve the Blackjack Oak acorn porridge warm, garnished with a sprinkle of cinnamon or nutmeg if desired.

Pecan Pie Bars

Prep Time: 45 minutes

Servings: 12

Ingredients:

- 1 cup all-purpose flour
- 1/2 cup unsalted butter, softened
- 1/4 cup powdered sugar
- 1/4 teaspoon salt
- 2 large eggs
- 3/4 cup dark corn syrup
- 1/2 cup granulated sugar
- 2 tablespoons unsalted butter, melted
- 1 teaspoon vanilla extract
- 1 1/2 cups pecan halves

Directions:

1. Preheat your oven to 350°F and line a 9-inch square baking pan with parchment paper.
2. Whisk together the flour, powdered sugar, and salt in a mixing bowl. Add the softened butter and use a pastry blender to cut it into the flour mixture until it resembles coarse crumbs.
3. Press the mixture evenly into the prepared baking pan, and bake for 18-20 minutes or until it is lightly golden brown.
4. While the crust is baking, prepare the filling. In a mixing bowl, whisk together the eggs, corn syrup, granulated sugar, melted butter, and vanilla extract until well combined.
5. Stir in the pecan halves, and mix until they are evenly coated in the filling.
6. Once the crust is finished baking, remove it from the oven and pour the filling over the top, spreading it out evenly with a spatula.
7. Bake for an additional 25-30 minutes or until the filling is set and the edges are golden brown.
8. Let the pecan pie bars cool completely in the pan, then slice them into squares and serve.

Enjoy!

Honey Mesquite Grilled Chicken

Prep Time: 10 minutes - Cook Time: 15 minutes

Servings: 4

Ingredients:

- 4 boneless, skinless chicken breasts
- 1/4 cup honey
- 1/4 cup soy sauce
- 2 tablespoons olive oil
- 2 tablespoons honey mesquite seasoning
- Salt and pepper to taste

Instructions:

1. Preheat the grill to medium-high heat.
2. Whisk together honey, soy sauce, olive oil, honey mesquite seasoning, salt, and pepper in a small bowl.
3. Place chicken breasts on a plate and pour the marinade over the chicken, making sure it is evenly coated.
4. Let the chicken marinate for at least 10 minutes or up to 1 hour.
5. Remove the chicken from the marinade and discard the remaining marinade.
6. Grill the chicken for 6-8 minutes per side or until the internal temperature reaches 165°F.

Note: You can also bake the chicken in the oven at 400°F for 20-25 minutes or until the internal temperature reaches 165°F.

Serve hot, and enjoy!

Roasted Screwbean Mesquite Pods

Prep time: 10 minutes - Cook time: 20 minutes

Servings: 4

Ingredients:

- 1 pound Screwbean Mesquite pods
- 2 tablespoons olive oil
- Salt and pepper to taste

Instructions:

1. Preheat the oven to 400°F (200°C).
2. Rinse the Screwbean Mesquite pods under running water and pat them dry with a paper towel.
3. Cut the pods into bite-sized pieces and place them in a mixing bowl.
4. Drizzle olive oil over the pods and toss them until evenly coated.
5. Season with salt and pepper to taste.
6. Spread the seasoned Screwbean Mesquite pods in a single layer on a baking sheet.
7. Roast the pods in the preheated oven for 20 minutes or until tender and slightly charred.
8. Remove from the oven and let them cool for a few minutes before serving.

Enjoy the roasted Screwbean Mesquite pods as a healthy and flavorful snack or side dish.

Sautéed Chicken of the Woods

Prep Time: 10 minutes - Cook Time: 15 minutes

Servings: 4

Ingredients:

- 1 pound chicken of the woods mushroom
- 2 tablespoons olive oil
- 1 tablespoon butter
- 2 cloves garlic, minced
- Salt and pepper, to taste
- Fresh parsley, chopped (optional)

Instructions:

1. Clean the chicken of the woods mushroom by wiping it with a damp cloth or brush. Cut it into bite-sized pieces.
2. In a large skillet, heat olive oil and butter over medium-high heat.
3. Add garlic and cook for 1-2 minutes until fragrant.
4. Add the chicken of the woods mushroom pieces to the skillet and season with salt and pepper to taste.
5. Cook the mushroom pieces for 10-12 minutes, stirring occasionally until they are tender and lightly browned.
6. Remove from heat and sprinkle with fresh parsley if desired.

Serve hot, and enjoy!

This Chicken of the Woods recipe can be enjoyed as a side dish or as a vegetarian main dish. It's a great way to enjoy this delicious mushroom's unique flavor and texture.

I ndigo Milkcap Sauté

This mushroom has a sweet and nutty flavor and can be used in a variety of dishes.

Preparation time: 15 minutes

Cooking time: 15 minutes

Ingredients:

- 1 pound Indigo Milkcap mushrooms, cleaned and sliced
- 2 tablespoons olive oil
- 2 cloves garlic, minced
- 1/2 teaspoon salt
- 1/4 teaspoon black pepper
- 1 tablespoon chopped fresh parsley

Instructions:

1. Heat the olive oil in a large skillet over medium-high heat.
2. Add the sliced Indigo Milkcap mushrooms to the skillet and cook for about 10 minutes, stirring occasionally, until the mushrooms are tender and lightly browned.
3. Add the minced garlic, salt, and black pepper to the skillet and continue cooking for an additional 2-3 minutes, stirring frequently, until the garlic is fragrant and lightly browned.
4. Remove the skillet from the heat and sprinkle the chopped fresh parsley over the mushrooms.
5. Serve the Indigo Milkcap sauté immediately as a side dish or as a topping for steak, pasta, or pizza.

Enjoy your delicious Indigo Milkcap sauté!

Lion's Mane Mushroom Stir Fry

Prep Time: 10 minutes - Cook Time: 15 minutes

Servings: 4

Ingredients:

- 1 lb fresh Lion's Mane mushrooms, sliced into 1/4 inch thick pieces
- 1 red bell pepper, sliced
- 1 green bell pepper, sliced
- 1 yellow onion, sliced
- 3 garlic cloves, minced
- 2 tbsp soy sauce
- 1 tbsp hoisin sauce
- 1 tbsp cornstarch
- 1 tbsp sesame oil
- 1 tbsp vegetable oil
- Salt and pepper to taste
- 2 green onions, sliced (optional)

Instructions:

1. Mix soy sauce, hoisin sauce, cornstarch, and 1/4 cup of water in a small bowl. Set aside.
2. Heat vegetable oil in a wok or large skillet over high heat. Add Lion's Mane mushrooms and stir-fry for 2-3 minutes until they start to brown. Remove from pan and set aside.
3. Add sesame oil to the same pan and stir-fry bell peppers and onion for 3-4 minutes until they are slightly tender.
4. Add garlic and stir-fry for another minute.
5. Add the sauce mixture to the pan and stir until it thickens.
6. Add the Lion's Mane mushrooms back into the pan and stir until everything is coated in the sauce.
7. Season with salt and pepper to taste.
8. Top with sliced green onions (optional) and serve hot.

This Lion's Mane Mushroom Stir Fry is a quick and easy recipe that is perfect for a healthy weeknight dinner. Enjoy!

S now Fungus Soup with Red Dates and Goji Berries

Prep Time: 10 minutes - Cook Time: 1 hour

Servings: 4-6

Ingredients:

- 30g snow fungus (also known as white fungus)
- 10 red dates (also known as jujubes)
- 2 tablespoons goji berries
- 1 liter water
- 1 rock sugar (optional)

Instructions:

1. Rinse the snow fungus in cold water and soak it in hot water for 15 minutes or until softened.
2. Cut off the hard parts and trim the edges of the snow fungus. Tear into smaller pieces.
3. Rinse the red dates and goji berries.
4. In a pot, bring 1 liter of water to a boil.
5. Add the snow fungus, red dates, and goji berries to the pot.
6. Reduce the heat to low and simmer for 1 hour.
7. If desired, add a rock sugar to taste.

Serve hot.

Note: Snow fungus is a type of mushroom that is commonly used in Chinese cuisine. It has a slightly crunchy texture and a mild, nutty flavor. This soup is believed to have various health benefits, including improving skin health and promoting relaxation.

Angel Hair Pasta with Wine Cap Mushrooms

Prep Time: 15 minutes - Cook Time: 20 minutes

Servings: 4

Ingredients:

- 8 oz. angel hair pasta
- 1/4 cup olive oil
- 1/2 cup finely chopped onion
- 3 garlic cloves, minced
- 1/2 tsp. red pepper flakes
- 8 oz. Wine Cap mushrooms, sliced
- 1/2 cup dry white wine
- 1/2 cup chicken broth
- 2 tbsp. unsalted butter
- 1/4 cup chopped fresh parsley
- 1/4 cup grated Parmesan cheese
- Salt and pepper to taste

Instructions:

1. Cook the angel hair pasta according to package instructions until al dente. Drain and set aside.
2. In a large skillet, heat the olive oil over medium heat. Add the onion and cook until softened about 3-4 minutes.
3. Add the garlic and red pepper flakes and cook for an additional 1-2 minutes.
4. Add the sliced Wine Cap mushrooms and cook for 5-7 minutes until the mushrooms release their moisture and start to brown.
5. Pour in the white wine and chicken broth and bring to a simmer. Cook for 5-7 minutes until the liquid has reduced by half.
6. Add the butter to the pan and stir until melted and well combined.
7. Add the cooked angel hair pasta to the pan and toss to coat in the mushroom sauce.
8. Stir in the chopped parsley and grated Parmesan cheese. Season with salt and pepper to taste.

Serve hot, and enjoy!

AFTERWORD

As I reflect on the journey of researching and writing this book on wild edible plants of Texas, I am struck by the immense diversity and richness of this region's natural bounty. From the rugged coastline to the soaring mountains, Texas is home to an incredible array of edible plants that have sustained human communities for thousands of years.

It has been a privilege to delve into these plants' history, folklore, and traditional uses and learn about their nutritional and medicinal properties. I hope this book has helped deepen your appreciation of the wild edible plants of Texas and perhaps inspired you to explore these foods for yourself.

Of course, as with any foraging activity, it is important to approach wild edible plants with caution and respect. It is crucial to correctly identify the plants you are harvesting, to gather them from safe and sustainable locations, and to avoid over-harvesting. It is also essential to be aware of any potential allergens or toxins that may be present in certain plants.

As you embark on your foraging adventures, I encourage you to seek knowledgeable guides and resources to help you navigate the rich and complex world of wild edible plants. Take the time to develop your skills and knowledge, and always approach these plants with a sense of wonder and gratitude for the abundance they provide.

Finally, I want to acknowledge the many Indigenous communities whose deep knowledge and relationship with the land have been instrumental in shaping our understanding of wild edible plants in Texas. I hope this book can serve as a small tribute to their wisdom and resilience and a reminder of the ongoing need to honor and respect Indigenous knowledge and sovereignty.

Thank you for joining me on this journey, and happy foraging!

If you enjoyed this book and found it a helpful guide and tool, leave a review for "Wild Edible Plants of Texas" on Amazon and share your thoughts and experiences with the world. Who knows - you could introduce someone to a new world of adventure and exploration.

PART TEN
APPENDIX

THE UNIVERSAL EDIBILTY TEST

If you are in an unfamiliar area or a survival situation, you may be unable to identify edible plants. In this case, you'd want to use the universal edibility test. As the name suggests, this test will help determine whether a plant is edible. It should only be used as a last resort, as you should ideally never be in a situation where you can't find an identifiable plant or mushroom. Always check the edibility of your harvest, even if you're sure it's safe to eat. This is important when foraging and Identify an edible plant you've never tried before.

Everyone will come across this scenario at some point. Even if you're confident that you've identified an edible plant, only try a small amount first. Even something safe to eat can make you feel unwell if you have issues with your digestion. Sometimes a food you haven't tried before doesn't agree with you, and you don't want to discover this after having a large portion. It's also possible to have an undiagnosed food allergy. Suppose you eat a lot of plant food on an empty stomach. In that case, you can quickly end up with cramps, nausea, diarrhea, or other gastrointestinal issues. An upset stomach is a quick way to ruin an otherwise enjoyable foraging trip.

Step 1: Fast for eight hours. You likely haven't eaten for at least eight hours in a survival situation like this. Still, it's essential to start on an empty stomach so that you know whether or not the plant you are testing is what has made you unwell. You can and should drink plenty of clean water, if possible.

Step 2: Check for common poisonous traits. Most toxic plants have distinguishing characteristics that are unlikely to be found on edible plants. These include shiny, waxy leaves, spines, fine hairs, milky sap, umbrella-shaped flowers, and green or white berries. If it looks like dill or parsley, avoid it, and steer clear of anything that smells like almonds. Not every plant with these characteristics is toxic, edible dandelions have milky sap, for example, but it's an excellent rule of thumb. Rule out anything with those traits.

Step 3: Once you find a plant without any of those traits, ensure you can find plenty of specimens. Remember, the edibility test takes time, so there's not much point in going through the whole process if you can't find any more plants of that type. When you find a likely plant, break it down into separate sections, flower, leaf, stem, etc. Not every plant part is edible, even if one part is. For example, potato tubers are edible, but the plant's stem is toxic. You will need to test every aspect of the plant individually.

Step 4: Now, it's time to start testing. Select a plant part and rub it on your skin. Most people rub it on their inner forearm, the inside of their elbow, or their outer lip. Wait for fifteen minutes. If you don't experience tingling, burning, or other adverse reactions, continue with the test. If any of the above persist, you will want to choose a different plant part.

Step 5: If all is well from the step above, do a taste test with the same plant part. Put it in your mouth and don't chew or swallow; just leave it for five minutes. Spit it out and wash your mouth if you have any adverse reactions. Do the same if you taste bitterness, soapy flavors, or experience numbness. If nothing happens, continue with the test.

Step 6: Do a more extensive taste test. Now put the plant part in your mouth and chew for five minutes. Wait for any of the adverse effects mentioned above and spit out excess saliva (don't swallow anything yet). If everything seems okay after five minutes, swallow the plant part. Now the waiting begins. You need to fast for another eight hours before the next step.

Step 7: If you haven't experienced any digestive issues, you can prepare and eat one tablespoon of the plant part. If possible, it's usually safer to cook the plant part. If there are no poisoning symptoms after another eight hours of waiting, you can be sure that this plant part is edible as you prepared. It would be best if you still didn't gorge yourself, but at least you have a relatively dependable food source. You'll reduce the chance of accidental poisoning by sticking with small amounts and waiting eight hours between tasting and eating. Suppose you have significant gastrointestinal symptoms in a survival situation, like vomiting or diarrhea. In that case, you may not be able to seek medical attention.

GLOSSARY

Plant Families

Actinidiaceae - This flowering plant family has three genera and about 355 species. They consist of shrubs, small trees, and lianas. They are primarily tropical and are particularly common in Southeast Asia.

Anacardiaceae - The cashew or sumac family of flowering plants includes 83 genera and 860 species. Several species bear drupes and sometimes produce *urushiol*, which can cause skin irritation.

Apiaceae - Known as the celery, carrot, and parsley family, or umbellifers, primarily aromatic flowering plants are named after the genus Apium.

Araliaceae - There are approximately 43 genera and about 1500 species of flowering plants in this family, most of these plants are woody, and some are herbaceous.

Asparagaceae - the asparagus family of flowering plants based on the edible garden asparagus, *Asparagus officinalis*.

Aspleniaceae - The spleenwort family **is** a family of ferns

Asteraceae - The Compositae family was first described in the year 1740. They are called daisies, sunflowers, asters, composites, or sunflowers. With more than 32,000 species and 1,900 genera, it is the world's largest flowering plant group, rivaled only by the Orchidaceae family.

Berberidaceae - Generally known as the Barberry family, this group of flowering plants contains 18 genera.

Brassicaceae - These medium-sized flowering plants are economically important. They are commonly known as the mustards, crucifers, or cabbage family.

Caryophyllaceae - The carnation family is a family of flowering plants with about 2,625 known species.

Elaeagnaceae - The Oleaster family comprises small trees and shrubs.

Ericaceae - The heath or heather family consists of flowering plants that flourish in acidic and infertile environments. Cranberries, blueberries, huckleberries, rhododendron (including azaleas), and a wide range of heaths and heathers are examples of well-known members.

Euphorbiaceae - Among flowering plants, the spurge family is one of the largest. They are also commonly known as euphorbias in English, their genus name. Most spurges are herbs, such as Euphorbia paralias, but some are shrubs or trees, particularly in the tropics.

Lamiaceae [LAY-mee-AY-see-ee] The mint or deadnettle family is aromatic in all parts. They include widely used culinary herbs like basil, mint, rosemary, sage, savory, marjoram, oregano, hyssop, thyme, lavender, and perilla. Catnip, salvia, bee balm, wild dagga, and oriental motherwort are medicinal herbs.

Malvaceae - The Mallow family of flowering plants is estimated to contain 244 genera with 4225 known species. Among the well-known members of this plant family are okra, cotton, cacao, and durian.

Menispermaceae - **The moonseed family** comprises 440 species, most of which are found in low-lying tropical regions, with some species also found in temperate and arid regions.

Morchellaceae -

Oxalidaceae - The wood sorrel family comprises five genera of herbaceous plants, shrubs, and small trees, with about 570 species in the Oxalis genus.

Plantaginaceae - The Plantain family and order Lamiales include common flower species such as snapdragon and foxglove.

Polygonaceae - The knotweed or smartweed-buckwheat family is an informal name for a family of flowering plants. There are about 1200 species within about 48 genera. There are members of this family worldwide, but they are most abundant in the North Temperate Zone.

Portulacaceae - The purslane family is a family of flowering plants with 115 species in one genus, Portulaca.

Ranunculaceae - the buttercup or crowfoot family is a family of over 2,000 known flowering plants in 43 genera distributed worldwide.

Rosaceae - The rose family includes 4,828 species of flowering plants.

Tremellaceae -

Viburnaceae - was previously known as the Adoxaceae family and is commonly known as the Moschatel family. About 150–200 species belong to this family of flowering plants.

Plant Types

Annual [AN-YOO-*UHL*] - Plants without a permanent woody stem. They are usually flowering garden plants or potherbs.

Deciduous [DIH-**SIJ**-OO-UHS] - After the growing season, the plant sheds leaves and turns dormant.

Dioecious [DAHY-EE-SH*UH*S] - having the male and female organs in separate and distinct individuals, having different sexes.

Herbaceous [HUR-**BEY**-SH*UH*S] - low-growing plants with soft green stems. Their aboveground growth is often seasonal.

Monoecious [MUH-**NEE**-SHUHS] - having the stamens and the pistils in separate flowers on the same plant.

Perennial [PUH-**REN**-EE-UHL] - It usually lasts for more than two years. These plants don't have a lot of woody growth.

Plant Parts

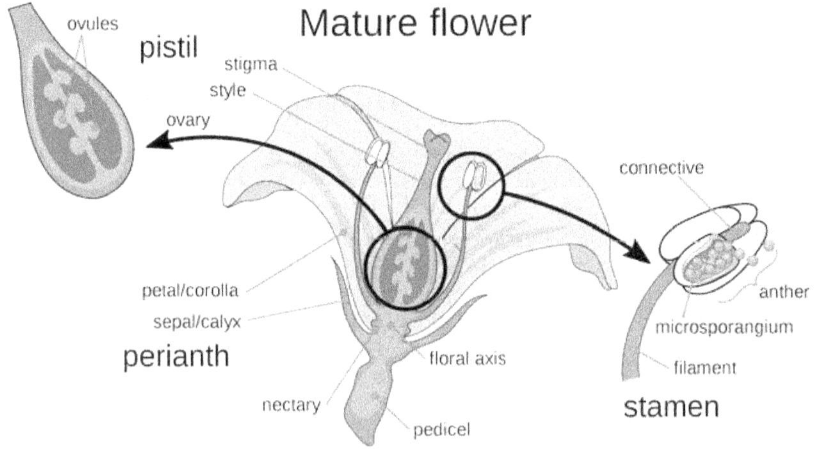

Achene [*uh*-ᴋᴇᴇɴ] - a small, dry one-seeded fruit that does not open to release the seed.

Anther [ᴀɴ-ᴛʜᴇʀ] - the pollen-bearing part of a stamen.

Filament [ꜰɪʟ-*uh*-ᴍᴜʜɴᴛ] - the stalklike portion of a stamen, supporting the anther.

Ligulate [ʟɪɢ-ʏᴜʜ-ʟɪᴛ] - strap-shaped, such as the ray florets of daisy family plants.

Peltate [ᴘᴇʟ-ᴛᴇʏᴛ] - fixed to the stalk by the center or by some point distinctly within the margin.

Petiole [ᴘᴇᴛ-ᴇᴇ-ᴏʜʟ] - the slender stalk by which a leaf is attached to the stem; leafstalk.

Pistil [ᴘɪs-ᴛʟ] - the ovule-bearing or seed-bearing female organ of a flower, consisting when complete of the ovary, style, and stigma.

Pith [ᴘɪᴛʜ] - The soft central cylinder of tissue in the plant's stem.

Sepal [sᴇᴇ-ᴘᴜʜʟ] - The outer parts of the flower (often green and leaf-like) that enclose a developing bud.

Sessile [sᴇs-ɪʟ] - attached directly by its base without a stalk or peduncle.

Stamen [sᴛᴇʏ-ᴍᴜʜɴ] - the pollen-bearing organ of a flower, consisting of the filament and the anther.

Staminodia [sᴛᴀᴍ-*uh*-ɴᴏʜ-ᴅᴇᴇ-*uh*] - A stamen that is sterile or abortive.

Whorled [ᴡᴜʀʟ'ᴅ] - The arrangement of like parts around a point on an axis, such as leaves or flowers;

Leaf Types

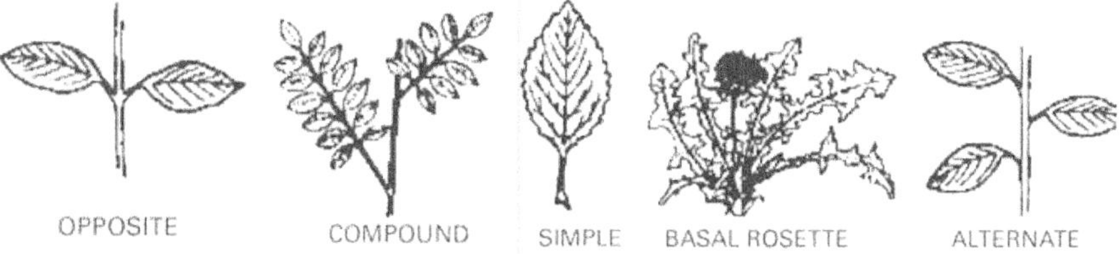

Alternate - The leaves are single at each node and spiral upwards along the stem.

Basal leaf - a leaf that grows lowest on the stem of a plant or flower.

Compound -

Opposite -

Palmate [ᴘᴀʟ-ᴍᴇʏᴛ] - Having four or more lobes or leaflets.

Palmately compound - A petiole's tip is attached to a leaflet.

Pinnate [ᴘɪɴ-ᴇʏᴛ] - Each side of a stalk is divided into leaflets

Rosette [ʀᴏʜ-ᴢᴇᴛ] - a circular arrangement of leaves or structures resembling leaves.

Simple - Leaves with a single, undivided lamina

Tripinnately compound - Leaf made up of three pinnate parts.

Leaf Shapes

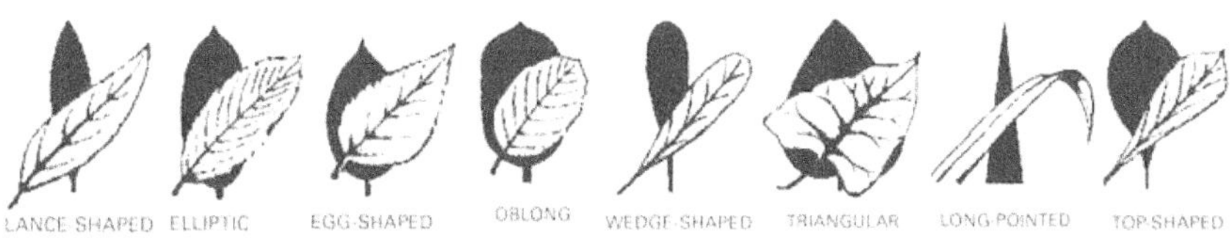

Cordate [ᴋᴀᴡʀ-ᴅᴇʏᴛ] - heart-shaped.

Elliptical [IH-**LIP**-TI-K*UHL*] - Planar, shaped like a flattened circle, symmetrical about the long and short axes, tapering equally to the tip and the base; oval.

Lanceolate [**AN**-SEE-*UH*-LEYT] - shaped like the head of a lance, having a rounded base and a tapering apex.

Long-pointed - Lying close and flat and pointing toward the plant's apex or structure.

Oblanceolate [OB-**LAN**-SEE-*UH*-LIT] - having a rounded apex and a tapering base.

Oblong [OB-LAWNG]- Having a length a few times greater than the width, with sides almost parallel and ends rounded.

Ovate [OH-VEYT] - egg-shaped, having such a shape with a broader end at the base.

Triangular [TRAHY-**ANG**-GY*UH*-LER] - Planar with three sides.

Wedge - narrowly triangular, wider at the apex, and tapering toward the base.

Flower Types

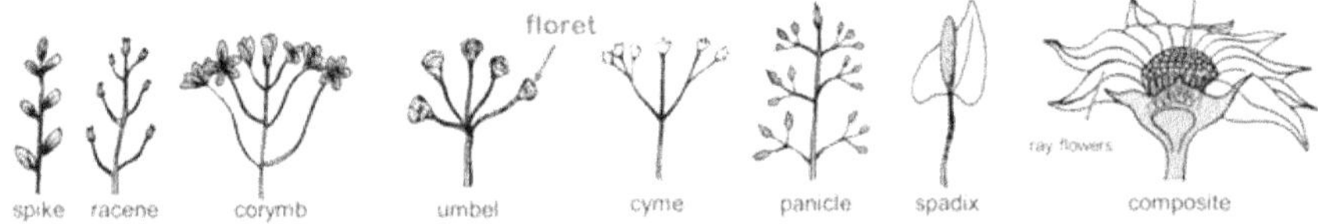

Corymb [KAWR-IMB] - a form of inflorescence in which the flowers form a flat-topped or convex cluster, the outermost flowers being the first to open.

Composite [KUHM-**POZ**-IT] is characterized by alternate, opposite, or *whorled* leaves and a whorl of bracts surrounding its flower heads. These flower heads typically extend from a disk containing tiny petal-less flowers and from the disk's rim to a ray of petals.

Cyme [SAHYM] - an inflorescence in which the primary axis bears a single central or terminal flower that blooms first.

Inflorescence [IN-**FLAW**-**RES**-*UH*NS] - the complete flower head of a plant, including stems, stalks, bracts, and flowers.

Panicle [**PAN**-I-K*UHL*] - any loose, diversely branching flower cluster.

Raceme [REY-SEEM] - a flower cluster with separate flowers attached by short equal stalks at equal distances along a central stem. The flowers at the base of the main stem develop first.

Spike [SPAHYK] - a type of racemose inflorescence.

Spadix [SPEY-DIKS] - an inflorescence consisting of a spike with a fleshy or thickened axis, usually enclosed in a spathe.

Umbel or Subumbel [UHM-B*UHL*] - consisting of several short flower stalks that spread from a common point, like umbrella ribs.

Fruit/Berry

Aggregate fruit [AG-RI-GIT FROOT]- composed of a cluster of carpels belonging to the same flower as the raspberry.

Dehiscent [D*□*'H*□*S*Ə*NT] - opens to release seeds or pollen

Drupe [DROOP] - a fleshy fruit with thin skin and a central stone containing the seed, e.g., a plum, cherry, almond, or olive.

Elaiosome [EH-LAY-UH-SOHM] - an oil-rich body on seeds or fruits that attract ants and act as dispersal agents.

Globoid [GLOH-BOID] - approximately globular. Globe-shaped; spherical.

Infructescence [IN-FRUC-**TES**-CENCE] - an aggregate fruit.

Myrmecochory [MIR-MI-KAW-KUH-REE] - the dispersal of fruits and seeds by ants.

Syconium [SAHY-KOH-NEE-*UHM*] - a fleshy hollow receptacle that develops into a multifruit.

Bark & Roots

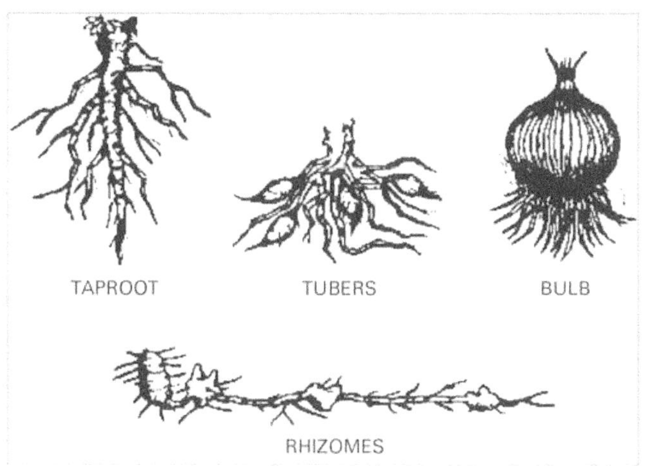

Acaulescent [AK-AW-LES-*UHNT*] - stemless

Lenticel [LEN-*TUH*-SEL] - One of the many holes in a woody plant's stem that allows air to exchange between the inside and outside.

Medical Terms

Amygdalin [*UH*-MIG-*DUH*-LIN] - White, bitter-tasting glycosidic powder usually obtained from the leaves and seeds of plants of the genus Prunus and related genera: used mainly as an expectorant in medicine.

Anthocyanins [AN-THUH-SAHY-UH-NIN] - These flavonoids are known for their pigmentation properties, responsible for fruits, vegetables, flowers, and cereals' red, purple, and blue colors.

Astringent [*UH*-STRIN-*JUHNT*] - Contracting the body's tissues or canals reduces mucus or blood discharges.

Berberine [BUR-*BUH*-REEN] - Known as an antipyretic, antibacterial, and stomachic, this crystalline, water-soluble alkaloid is derived from barberry or goldenseal.

Carotenoid [*KUH*-ROT-N-OID] - Red or yellow pigments, similar to carotene, found in animal fat and some plants.

Cyanogenic glycosides - chemical compounds contained in foods that release hydrogen cyanide when chewed or digested.

Demulcent [DIH-MUHL-SU*HNT*] - a substance that relieves irritation of the mucous membranes in the mouth by forming a protective film.

Depurative [DEP-*YUH*-REY-TIV] - herbs considered to have purifying and detoxifying effects.

Flavonoids [FLEY-VUH-NOID] - An antioxidant, antiviral, anticancer, anti-inflammatory, and anti-allergenic group of water-soluble polyphenols found in plants.

Hydrocyanic acid - scientific word for cyanide.

Lycopene [LAHY-KUH-PEEN] - Red crystalline substance found in some fruits, including tomatoes and paprika.

Odontalgic [OH-DON-TAL-JUH] - toothache.

Prunasin [PRÜ-Nə-SəN] - A cyanogenic glucoside related to amygdalin found in Prunus species.

Urolithiasis [YOOR-OH-LI-THAHY-UH-SIS] - A disease where stones form in the urinary tract.

Urushiol [OO-ROO-SHEE-AWL] - The active irritant principle in several plant species in the Rhus genus.

General definitions

Anthropogenic [AN-THRUH-PUH-JEN-IK] - caused by humans.

Glaucous [GLAW-KUHS] - covered with a whitish bloom, as a plum.

Siliceous [SUH-LISH-UHS] - growing in soil rich in silica.

Calcareous [KAL-KAIR-EE-UHS] - occurring on chalk or limestone.

Monoecious [MUH-NEE-SHUHS] - THE STAMENS AND PISTILS ARE IN SEPARATE FLOWERS ON THE SAME PLANT.

Mucilaginous [MYOO-SUH-LAJ-UH-NUHS] - having a viscous or gelatinous consistency.

PLANT INDEX

Agarita ____ 71
American Beautyberry _____________________________________ 73
American Beech ____ 51
Artist's Conk ____ 151
Black Hickory ____ 133
Black Walnut ____ 53
Blackjack Oak ____ 135
Blue Vervain ____ 101
Bracken Fern ____ 175
Broadleaf Cattail ____ 103
Castor Bean ____ 177
Chanterelle ____ 57
Chicken of the Woods ______________________________________ 59
Chickweed ____ 39
Chicory ____ 41
Chinaberry ____ 176
Common Hackberry _______________________________________ 137
Dandelion ____ 43
Devil's Cigar ____ 153
Dryad Saddle ____ 155
Edwards Plateau Pecan ____________________________________ 139
Enoki ____ 157
Evening Primrose ____ 105
Farkleberry ____ 75
Flameleaf Sumac ____ 77
Greater Mullein ____ 107
Grey Knight ____ 161
Horsemint ____ 109
Indian Fig ____ 79
Indian Rice Grass ____ 113
Indigo Milkcap ____ 159
Inland Sea Oats ____ 111
King Bolete ____ 61
Lemon Balm ____ 117
Lobster ____ 63
Mallow ____ 45
Mayhaw ____ 81

Mesquite ____141
Mexican Oregano ____119
Mustang Grape ____83
Oleander ____175
Osage Orange ____143
Oyster ____65
Purple coneflower ____121
Purple Deadnettle ____47
Purslane ____49
Rosemary ____123
Sand Plum ____85
Short Stemmed Russula ____163
Snow Fungus ____165
Soapberry ____87
Southern Magnolia ____145
Spanish Daggerfruit ____89
Spotted Joe-Pye weed ____115
Straw Mushroom ____167
Sugar Hackberry ____37
Sweet Acacia ____91
Texas Mountain Laurel ____176
Texas Persimmon ____93
Western Giant Puffball ____169
Western Wheatgrass ____127
White Morel ____67
White Oak ____55
Wild Blue Larkspur ____178
Wine Cap ____171
Yarrow ____125
Yaupon Holly ____97
Yellow Jessamine ____177
Yellow Passionfruit ____95

BIBLIOGRAPHY

Photo Attribution

Rubus allegheniensis Porter observed in the United States of America by Sandy Wolkenberg (licensed under http://creativecommons.org/licenses/by/4.0/)

Rubus allegheniensis Porter observed in the United States of America by Andrew Garn (licensed under http://creativecommons.org/licenses/by/4.0/)

Sambucus canadensis L. observed in the United States of America by Kim (licensed under http://creativecommons.org/licenses/by/4.0/)

Sambucus canadensis L. observed in the United States of America by mfeaver (licensed under http://creativecommons.org/licenses/by/4.0/)

Rosa canina L. observed in the United States of America by Chris Johnson (licensed under http://creativecommons.org/licenses/by/4.0/)

Stellaria media (L.) Vill. observed in the United States of America by giantcicada (licensed under http://creativecommons.org/licenses/by/4.0/)

Stellaria media (L.) Vill. observed in the United States of America by Randy A Nonenmacher (licensed under http://creativecommons.org/licenses/by/4.0/)

Lippia graveolens Kunth observed in the United States of America by CK Kelly (licensed under http://creativecommons.org/licenses/by/4.0/)

Lippia graveolens Kunth observed in the United States of America by johnyochum licensed under http://creativecommons.org/licenses/by/4.0/)

Lippia graveolens Kunth observed in Mexico by Neptalí Ramírez Marcial (licensed under http://creativecommons.org/licenses/by/4.0/)

Lippia graveolens Kunth observed in Mexico by Sula Vanderplank (licensed under http://creativecommons.org/licenses/by/4.0/)

Chorioactis geaster (Peck) Kupfer ex Eckblad observed in the United States of America by Richard Jacob (licensed under http://creativecommons.org/licenses/by/4.0/)

Chorioactis geaster (Peck) Kupfer ex Eckblad observed in the United States of America by Michelle (licensed under http://creativecommons.org/licenses/by/4.0/)

Chorioactis geaster (Peck) Kupfer ex Eckblad observed in the United States of America by Michelle (licensed under http://creativecommons.org/licenses/by/4.0/)

Chorioactis geaster (Peck) Kupfer ex Eckblad observed in the United States of America by Annika Lindqvist (licensed under http://creativecommons.org/licenses/by/4.0/)

Chorioactis geaster (Peck) Kupfer ex Eckblad observed in the United States of America by Annika Lindqvist (licensed under http://creativecommons.org/licenses/by/4.0/)

References

Acacia farnesiana Sweet Acacia, Perfume Acacia, Huisache PFAF Plant Database. (n.d.). https://pfaf.org/user/Plant.aspx?LatinName=Acacia+farnesiana

Achillea millefolium - Plant Finder. (n.d.). https://www.missouribotanicalgarden.org/PlantFinder/PlantFinderDetails.aspx?kempercode=b282

Achillea millefolium (common yarrow):   Go Botany. (n.d.). https://gobotany.nativeplanttrust.org/species/achillea/millefolium/

Achillea millefolium (Common Yarrow): Minnesota Wildflowers. (n.d.). https://www.minnesotawildflowers.info/flower/common-yarrow

Achillea millefolium Yarrow, Boreal yarrow, California yarrow, Giant yarrow, Coast yarrow,

Western yarrow, Pacific yarrow PFAF Plant Database. (n.d.). https://pfaf.org/user/plant.aspx?LatinName=Achillea+millefolium

Achnatherum hymenoides - FNA. (n.d.). http://floranorthamerica.org/Achnatherum_hymenoides

Achnatherum hymenoides Indian Millet, Indian ricegrass PFAF Plant Database. (n.d.). https://pfaf.org/user/Plant.aspx?LatinName=Achnatherum+hymenoides

Achnatherum hymenoides (Indian Rice Grass): Minnesota Wildflowers. (n.d.). https://www.minnesotawildflowers.info/grass-sedge-rush/indian-rice-grass

Agriculture, Climate & Geography. (n.d.). Texas Film Commission | Office of the Governor | Greg Abbott. https://gov.texas.gov/film/page/agriculture_climate_geography#:~:text=Weather%20Information&text=The%20summers%20in%20Texas%20provide,as%20seasons%20begin%20to%20change.

American Beautyberry (Callicarpa americana). (n.d.). American Beautyberry (Callicarpa Americana). https://www.uaex.uada.edu/yard-garden/resource-library/plant-database/shrubs/american-beautyberry.aspx

Anps, W. (2020, November 29). Know Your Natives – Yellow Passionflower. Arkansas Native Plant Society. https://anps.org/2014/09/25/know-your-natives-yellow-passionflower/

Bautista-Hernández, I., Aguilar, C. N., Martínez-Ávila, G. C. G., Torres-León, C., Ilyina, A., Flores-Gallegos, A. C., Verma, D. K., & Chávez-González, M. L. (2021). Mexican Oregano (Lippia graveolens Kunth) as Source of Bioactive Compounds: A Review. Molecules, 26(17), 5156. https://doi.org/10.3390/molecules26175156

Black Hickory (Carya texana). (n.d.). https://www.illinoiswildflowers.info/trees/plants/bl_hickory.html

Blackjack Oak (Quercus marilandica). (n.d.). https://www.illinoiswildflowers.info/trees/plants/bj_oak.html

Callicarpa americana (American Beautyberry, American Mulberry, Beautyberry, French Mulberry, Sour-bush) | North Carolina Extension Gardener Plant Toolbox. (n.d.). https://plants.ces.ncsu.edu/plants/callicarpa-americana/

Callicarpa americana page. (n.d.). https://www.missouriplants.com/Callicarpa_americana_page.html

Calvatia booniana (Western Giant Puffball). (n.d.). Copyright (C) 2023 by coloradomushrooms.com. https://www.coloradomushrooms.com/mushroom.php?id=14

Carya illinoinensis | Landscape Plants | Oregon State University. (n.d.). https://landscapeplants.oregonstate.edu/plants/carya-illinoinensis

Carya illinoinensis - Plant Finder. (n.d.). https://www.missouribotanicalgarden.org/PlantFinder/PlantFinderDetails.aspx?kempercode=a852

Carya illinoinensis (Hardy Pecan, Pecan) | North Carolina Extension Gardener Plant Toolbox. (n.d.). https://plants.ces.ncsu.edu/plants/carya-illinoinensis/

Carya illinoinensis Pecan PFAF Plant Database. (n.d.). https://pfaf.org/user/Plant.aspx?LatinName=Carya+illinoinensis

Carya texana, black hickory. (n.d.). https://biosurvey.ou.edu/shrub/cate9.htm

Carya texana Black Hickory PFAF Plant Database. (n.d.). https://pfaf.org/USER/Plant.aspx?LatinName=Carya+texana

Celtis laevigata (Hackberry, Southern Hackberry, Sugarberry, Sugar Hackberry) | North Carolina Extension Gardener Plant Toolbox. (n.d.). https://plants.ces.ncsu.edu/plants/celtis-laevigata/

Celtis laevigata Sugarberry, Netleaf hackberry, Texan sugarberry, Sugar Hackberry PFAF Plant Database. (n.d.). https://pfaf.org/user/Plant.aspx?LatinName=Celtis+laevigata

Celtis occidentalis | Landscape Plants | Oregon State University. (n.d.). https://landscapeplants.oregonstate.edu/plants/celtis-occidentalis

Celtis occidentalis (American Hackberry, Beaverwood, Common Hackberry, False Elm, Hackberry, Nettle Tree, Northern Hackberry) | North Carolina Extension Gardener Plant Toolbox. (n.d.). https://plants.ces.ncsu.edu/plants/celtis-occidentalis/

Celtis occidentalis Hackberry, Common hackberry PFAF Plant Database. (n.d.). https://pfaf.org/user/Plant.aspx?LatinName=Celtis+occidentalis

Celtis occidentalis (Hackberry): Minnesota Wildflowers. (n.d.). https://www.minnesotawildflowers.info/tree/hackberry

Center for Aquatic and Invasive Plants | University of Florida, IFAS. (n.d.). https://plants.ifas.ufl.edu/plant-directory/lactarius-indigo/

Chasmanthium latifolium - Plant Finder. (n.d.). https://www.missouribotanicalgarden.org/PlantFinder/PlantFinderDetails.aspx?kempercode=a240

Chasmanthium latifolium (Indian Wood Oats, Inland Sea Oats, Northern Sea Oats, River Oats, Wild Oats, Wood-oat) | North Carolina Extension Gardener Plant Toolbox. (n.d.). https://plants.ces.ncsu.edu/plants/chasmanthium-latifolium/

Chasmanthium latifolium Indian Woodoats, Wild Oats Grass, North American Wild Oats, Northern Sea Oats, Spanglegrass River Oa PFAF Plant Database. (n.d.). https://pfaf.org/user/Plant.aspx?LatinName=Chasmanthium+latifolium

Common Evening Primrose (Oenothera biennis). (n.d.). https://www.illinoiswildflowers.info/prairie/plantx/cm_primrosex.htm

Common Hackberry (Celtis occidentalis). (n.d.). https://www.illinoiswildflowers.info/trees/plants/hackberry.html

common mullein, Verbascum thapsus Scrophulariales: Scrophulariaceae. (n.d.). https://www.invasive.org/browse/subinfo.cfm?sub=3080

Crataegus opaca - Species Details. (n.d.). Atlas of Florida Plants. https://florida.plantatlas.usf.edu/plant.aspx?id=4280

Crataegus opaca Western Mayhaw PFAF Plant Database. (n.d.). https://pfaf.org/user/plant.aspx?LatinName=Crataegus+opaca

Cywinski, R. (2019, August 8). Texas persimmon. Native Plant Society of Texas. https://npsot.org/wp/plant-profiles/texas-persimmon/11725/

Delphinium carolinianum (Blue Larkspur, Carolina Larkspur, Glade Larkspur, Pine Woods Larkspur, Prairie Larkspur) | North Carolina Extension Gardener Plant Toolbox. (n.d.). https://plants.ces.ncsu.edu/plants/delphinium-carolinianum/

Delphinium carolinianum (Carolina Larkspur): Minnesota Wildflowers. (n.d.). https://www.minnesotawildflowers.info/flower/carolina-larkspur

details. (n.d.). http://www.tsusinvasives.org/home/database/melia-azedarach

Dried Organic. (n.d.). Forest Mushrooms. https://www.forestmushrooms.com/products/dried-cauliflower-mushrooms-1

Echinacea purpurea - Plant Finder. (n.d.). https://www.missouribotanicalgarden.org/PlantFinder/PlantFinderDetails.aspx?kempercode=c580

Echinacea purpurea (Coneflower, Eastern Purple Coneflower, Purple Coneflower, Purple Rudbeckia) | North Carolina Extension Gardener Plant Toolbox. (n.d.). https://plants.ces.ncsu.edu/plants/echinacea-purpurea/

Echinacea purpurea (Eastern Purple Coneflower): Minnesota Wildflowers. (n.d.). https://www.minnesotawildflowers.info/flower/eastern-purple-coneflower

Echinacea purpurea Echinacea, Eastern purple coneflower, Hedge Coneflower, Black Sampson , Purple Coneflower PFAF Plant Database. (n.d.). https://pfaf.org/user/Plant.aspx?LatinName=Echinacea+purpurea

Elmer, N. L. (2019, September 12). The Trees of BFL: Sugarberry (Celtis laevigata). https://biodiversity.utexas.edu/news/entry/the-trees-of-bfl-sugarberry-celtis-laevigata

Eutrochium maculatum - Plant Finder. (n.d.). https://www.missouribotanicalgarden.org/PlantFinder/PlantFinderDetails.aspx?taxonid=292659

Eutrochium maculatum (Joe-Pye-weed, Queen of the Meadow, Spotted Joe-pye-weed, Spotted

Trumpet Weed) | North Carolina Extension Gardener Plant Toolbox. (n.d.). https://plants. ces.ncsu.edu/plants/eutrochium-maculatum/

Eutrochium maculatum (Spotted Joe-pye Weed): Minnesota Wildflowers. (n.d.). https://www. minnesotawildflowers.info/flower/spotted-joe-pye-weed

Find Trees & Learn | University of Arizona Campus Arboretum. (n.d.). https://apps.cals. arizona.edu/arboretum/taxon.aspx?id=777

Flammulina velutipes. (n.d.). https://www.messiah.edu/Oakes/fungi_on_wood/gilled% 20fungi/species%20pages/Flammulina%20velutipes.htm

Flammulina velutipes, aka winter mushroom, velvet stem, velvet foot, enoki, enokitake, Tom Volk's Fungus of the Month for March 1997. (n.d.). https://botit.botany.wisc.edu/toms_ fungi/march97.html

Florida Native Plant Society (FNPS). (n.d.-a). https://www.fnps.org/plant/vaccinium-arboreum

Florida Native Plant Society (FNPS). (n.d.-b). https://www.fnps.org/plant/prunus-angustifolia

Florida Native Plant Society (FNPS). (n.d.-c). https://www.fnps.org/plant/ilex-vomitoria

Florida Native Plant Society (FNPS). (n.d.-d). https://www.fnps.org/plant/chasmanthium-lati folium

Florida Native Plant Society (FNPS). (n.d.-e). https://www.fnps.org/plant/gelsemium-semper virens

From Woodlots to Landscapes: The Impressive Dryad's Saddle Polypore Fungus. (2019, May 24). BYGL. https://bygl.osu.edu/node/1279

Ganoderma applanatum, Artist's Fungus. (n.d.). https://www.first-nature.com/fungi/gano derma-applanatum.php

Gelsemium sempervirens - Plant Finder. (n.d.). https://www.missouribotanicalgarden.org/ PlantFinder/PlantFinderDetails.aspx?taxonid=282490

Gelsemium sempervirens - Species Details. (n.d.). Atlas of Florida Plants. https://florida.plantat las.usf.edu/plant.aspx?id=874

Gelsemium sempervirens (Carolina Jasmine, Carolina Jessamine, Carolina Yellow Jessamine, Yellow Jessamine) | North Carolina Extension Gardener Plant Toolbox. (n.d.). https://plants. ces.ncsu.edu/plants/gelsemium-sempervirens/

Gong, S., Chen, C., Zhu, J., Qi, G., & Jiang, S. (2018). Effects of wine-capStrophariacultivation on soil nutrients and bacterial communities in forestlands of northern China. PeerJ, 6, e5741. https://doi.org/10.7717/peerj.5741

Grass Species Detail Page. (n.d.). https://cals.arizona.edu/yavapaiplants/SpeciesDetailGrass. php?genus=Pascopyrum&species=smithii

Henciya, S., Seturaman, P., James, A. R., Tsai, Y., Nikam, R., Wu, Y. C., Dahms, H., & Chang, F. R. (2017). Biopharmaceutical potentials of Prosopis spp. (Mimosaceae, Leguminosa). Journal of Food and Drug Analysis, 25(1), 187–196. https://doi.org/10.1016/j.jfda.2016.11.001

Hossain, M. M., Barua, A., Tanim, M. a. H., Hasan, M. K., Islam, M. T., Hossain, M. R., Emon, N. U., & Hossen, S. M. M. (2021). Ganoderma applanatum mushroom provides new insights into the management of diabetes mellitus, hyperlipidemia, and hepatic degeneration: A comprehensive analysis. Food Science and Nutrition, 9(8), 4364–4374. https://doi.org/10.1002/fsn3.2407

Ilex vomitoria Yaupon Holly, PFAF Plant Database. (n.d.). https://pfaf.org/user/Plant.aspx? LatinName=Ilex+vomitoria

Ilex vomitoria (Yaupon, Yaupon Holly) | North Carolina Extension Gardener Plant Toolbox. (n.d.). https://plants.ces.ncsu.edu/plants/ilex-vomitoria/

JC Raulston Arboretum - Our Plants - Yucca treculeana. (n.d.). https://jcra.ncsu.edu/horticul ture/our-plants/results-by-name-serial-number.php?serial=105794

Klimaszyk, P., & Rzymski, P. (2018). The Yellow Knight Fights Back: Toxicological, Epidemiological, and Survey Studies Defend Edibility of Tricholoma equestre. Toxins, 10(11), 468. https:// doi.org/10.3390/toxins10110468

Lactarius indigo, the indigo milk mushroom, Tom Volk's Fungus of the Month for June 2000. (n.d.). https://botit.botany.wisc.edu/toms_fungi/june2000

Lady Bird Johnson Wildflower Center - The University of Texas at Austin. (n.d.-a). https://www.wildflower.org/plants/result.php?id_plant=veha2

Lady Bird Johnson Wildflower Center - The University of Texas at Austin. (n.d.-b). https://www.wildflower.org/plants/result.php?id_plant=tyla

Lady Bird Johnson Wildflower Center - The University of Texas at Austin. (n.d.-c). https://www.wildflower.org/plants/result.php?id_plant=tyla

Lady Bird Johnson Wildflower Center - The University of Texas at Austin. (n.d.-d). https://www.wildflower.org/plants/result.php?id_plant=tyla

Lady Bird Johnson Wildflower Center - The University of Texas at Austin. (n.d.-e). https://www.wildflower.org/plants/result.php?id_plant=OEBI

Lemon balm. (n.d.). Mount Sinai Health System. https://www.mountsinai.org/health-library/herb/lemon-balm

Lemon Bee Balm (Monarda citriodora). (n.d.). https://www.illinoiswildflowers.info/weeds/plants/lemon_bb.html

Lippia graveolens Mexican Oregano PFAF Plant Database. (n.d.). https://pfaf.org/user/Plant.aspx?LatinName=Lippia+graveolens

Ma, X., Yang, M., He, Y., Zhai, C., & Li, C. (2021). A review on the production, structure, bioactivities and applications of Tremella polysaccharides. International Journal of Immunopathology and Pharmacology, 35, 205873842110005. https://doi.org/10.1177/20587384211000541

Maclura pomifera | Landscape Plants | Oregon State University. (n.d.). https://landscapeplants.oregonstate.edu/plants/maclura-pomifera

Maclura pomifera - Plant Finder. (n.d.). https://www.missouribotanicalgarden.org/PlantFinder/PlantFinderDetails.aspx?kempercode=a879

Maclura pomifera (Osage Orange). (n.d.). https://www.illinoiswildflowers.info/trees/plants/osage_orange.htm

Maclura pomifera Osage Orange, Bois D'Arc PFAF Plant Database. (n.d.). https://pfaf.org/user/Plant.aspx?LatinName=Maclura+pomifera

Magnolia grandiflora | Landscape Plants | Oregon State University. (n.d.). https://landscapeplants.oregonstate.edu/plants/magnolia-grandiflora

Magnolia grandiflora - Plant Finder. (n.d.). https://www.missouribotanicalgarden.org/PlantFinder/PlantFinderDetails.aspx?kempercode=c117

Magnolia grandiflora Southern Magnolia, Bull Bay, Large-flowered Magnolia, Southern Magnolia PFAF Plant Database. (n.d.). https://pfaf.org/user/Plant.aspx?LatinName=Magnolia+grandiflora

Mahonia trifoliolata Mexican Barberry, Algerita PFAF Plant Database. (n.d.). https://pfaf.org/user/Plant.aspx?LatinName=Mahonia+trifoliolata

Maryland Biodiversity Project - Yellow Passionflower (Passiflora lutea). (n.d.). https://www.marylandbiodiversity.com/view/2172

Mckinley. (2021a). Vaccinium arboreum. Tennessee Smart Yards. https://tnyards.utk.edu/vaccinium-arboreum/

Mckinley. (2021b, February 18). Vaccinium arboreum. Tennessee Smart Yards. https://tnyards.utk.edu/vaccinium-arboreum/

Melia azedarach - Florida Natural Areas Inventory. (n.d.). https://www.fnai.org/species-communities/invasives/invasive-species?ID=103

Melia azedarach - Species Details. (n.d.). Atlas of Florida Plants. https://florida.plantatlas.usf.edu/plant.aspx?id=1691

Melia azedarach, chinaberry | Trees of Stanford & Environs. (n.d.). https://trees.stanford.edu/ENCYC/MELIAaz.htm

Melissa officinalis - Plant Finder. (n.d.). https://www.missouribotanicalgarden.org/Plant Finder/PlantFinderDetails.aspx?kempercode=c857

Melissa officinalis (Balm, Balm Mint, Common Balm, Lemon Balm) | North Carolina Extension Gardener Plant Toolbox. (n.d.). https://plants.ces.ncsu.edu/plants/melissa-officinalis/

Melissa officinalis Lemon Balm, Common balm, Bee Balm, Sweet Balm, Lemon Balm PFAF Plant Database. (n.d.). https://pfaf.org/user/plant.aspx?latinname=Melissa+officinalis

Miraj, S., Rafieian-Kopaei, & Kiani, S. (2017). Melissa officinalis L: A Review Study With an Antioxidant Prospective. Journal of Evidence-Based Complementary & Alternative Medicine, 22(3), 385–394. https://doi.org/10.1177/2156587216663433

Mocan, A., Fernandes, Â., Barros, L., Crişan, G., Ivanov, M., Soković, M., & Ferreira, I. C. (2018). Chemical composition and bioactive properties of the wild mushroom Polyporus squamosus (Huds.) Fr: a study with samples from Romania. Food & Function, 9(1), 160–170. https://doi.org/10.1039/c7fo01514c

Monarda citriodora - Plant Finder. (n.d.). https://www.missouribotanicalgarden.org/Plant Finder/PlantFinderDetails.aspx?taxonid=281493

Monarda citriodora Lemon Bergamot, Lemon beebalm. Lemon Mint PFAF Plant Database. (n.d.). https://pfaf.org/user/Plant.aspx?LatinName=Monarda+citriodora

Mountain, M. (2019). Enoki “Velvet Foot” – (Flammulina velutipes). Mushroom Mountain. https://mushroommountain.com/enoki-velvet-foot-flammulina-velutipes/

Mountain, M. (2021). How to Grow Paddy Straw Mushrooms – Volvariella volvacea. Mushroom Mountain. https://mushroommountain.com/how-to-grow-paddy-straw-mush rooms-volvariella-volvacea/

Mushroom. (2023). Giant Puffball Mushrooms: Identification, Foraging, and Recipes - Mushroom Appreciation. Mushroom Appreciation. https://www.mushroom-appreciation.com/puffball-mushrooms.html

MushroomExpert.Com. (n.d.-a). Calvatia booniana (MushroomExpert.Com). https://www.mushroomexpert.com/calvatia_booniana.html

MushroomExpert.Com. (n.d.-b). Chorioactis geaster (MushroomExpert.Com). https://www.mushroomexpert.com/chorioactis_geaster.html

MushroomExpert.Com. (n.d.-c). Ganoderma applanatum (MushroomExpert.Com). https://www.mushroomexpert.com/ganoderma_applanatum.html

MushroomExpert.Com. (n.d.-d). Lactarius indigo (MushroomExpert.Com). https://www.mushroomexpert.com/lactarius_indigo.html

MushroomExpert.Com. (n.d.-e). Polyporus squamosus (MushroomExpert.Com). https://www.mushroomexpert.com/polyporus_squamosus.html

MushroomExpert.Com. (n.d.-f). Russula brevipes (MushroomExpert.Com). https://www.mushroomexpert.com/russula_brevipes.html

MushroomExpert.Com. (n.d.-g). Stropharia rugosoannulata (MushroomExpert.Com). https://www.mushroomexpert.com/stropharia_rugosoannulata.html

MushroomExpert.Com. (n.d.-h). Tremella fuciformis (MushroomExpert.Com). https://www.mushroomexpert.com/tremella_fuciformis.html

MushroomExpert.Com. (n.d.-i). Tricholoma equestre (MushroomExpert.Com). https://www.mushroomexpert.com/tricholoma_equestre.html

MushroomExpert.Com. (n.d.-j). Volvariella volvacea (MushroomExpert.Com). https://www.mushroomexpert.com/volvariella_volvacea.html

MyCoPortal - Chorioactis geaster. (n.d.). https://www.mycoportal.org/portal/taxa/index.php?tid=553194

Nerium oleander - Plant Finder. (n.d.). https://www.missouribotanicalgarden.org/Plant Finder/PlantFinderDetails.aspx?kempercode=a532

Nerium oleander - Species Details. (n.d.). Atlas of Florida Plants. https://florida.plantatlas.usf.edu/plant.aspx?id=1725

Nerium oleander Oleander, Rose Bay PFAF Plant Database. (n.d.). https://pfaf.org/User/Plant.aspx?LatinName=Nerium+oleander

October 2003. (2011, February 12). Boerne Chapter of Native Plant Society of Texas. https://npsot.org/wp/boerne/plant-of-the-month/year-2003/oct-2003/

Oenothera biennis (Evening Primrose) | North Carolina Extension Gardener Plant Toolbox. (n.d.). https://plants.ces.ncsu.edu/plants/oenothera-biennis/

Oenothera biennis Evening Primrose, Sun Drop, Common evening primrose PFAF Plant Database. (n.d.). https://pfaf.org/user/Plant.aspx?LatinName=Oenothera+biennis

Online Plant Guide. (n.d.). Online Plant Guide - Crataegus opaca / Mayhaw. https://www.onlineplantguide.com/Plant-Details/678/

Opuntia ficus-indica | The Huntington. (n.d.). https://huntington.org/educators/learning-resources/spotlight/opuntia-ficus-indica

Opuntia ficus-indica Prickly Pear, Barbary fig PFAF Plant Database. (n.d.). https://pfaf.org/user/Plant.aspx?LatinName=Opuntia+ficus-indica

Opuntia ficus-indica, tree prickly pear cactus, fruit. (2020, October 2). Opuntia Web. https://www.opuntiads.com/opuntia-ficus-indica/

Orr, E. (2019, December 27). Yaupon holly (Ilex vomitoria): how to forage. Foraging for Wild Edibles. https://www.wildedible.com/wild-food-guide/yaupon-holly

Passiflora lutea - Species Details. (n.d.). Atlas of Florida Plants. https://florida.plantatlas.usf.edu/plant.aspx?id=3988

Passiflora lutea (Dwarf Passionflower, Eastern Yellow Passionflower, Hardy Yellow Passionflower, Passion flower) | North Carolina Extension Gardener Plant Toolbox. (n.d.). https://plants.ces.ncsu.edu/plants/passiflora-lutea/

Pinzone, P. (2019, February 1). Chorioactis geaster. Forest Floor Narrative. https://www.forestfloornarrative.com/blog/2019/2/1/chorioactis-geaster

Plant ID Guide:Western Wheatgrass (Pascopyrum smithii) - Kansas Native Plants. (n.d.). https://kansasnativeplants.com/guide/plant_detail.php?plnt_id=658

Plants of Texas Rangelands » Texas persimmon. (n.d.). https://rangeplants.tamu.edu/plant/texas-persimmon/

Polyporus squamosus. (2019, July 3). Midwest American Mycological Information. https://midwestmycology.org/polyporus-squamosus/

Prunus angustifolia - Species Page - APA: Alabama Plant Atlas. (n.d.). http://www.floraofalabama.org/Plant.aspx?id=3174

Prunus angustifolia (Chickasaw Plum) | North Carolina Extension Gardener Plant Toolbox. (n.d.). https://plants.ces.ncsu.edu/plants/prunus-angustifolia/

Prunus angustifolia Chickasaw Plum, Watson's plum, Hally Jolivette Cherry PFAF Plant Database. (n.d.). https://pfaf.org/user/Plant.aspx?LatinName=Prunus+angustifolia

Pteridium aquilinum - Plant Finder. (n.d.). https://www.missouribotanicalgarden.org/PlantFinder/PlantFinderDetails.aspx?taxonid=285684

Pteridium aquilinum (Adelaarsvaring, Bracken Fern, Brake, Brake Fern, Eagle Fern, Hog-Pasture Bracken, Pasture Bracken, Tailed Bracken Fern, Umbewe, Umhlashoshana) | North Carolina Extension Gardener Plant Toolbox. (n.d.). https://plants.ces.ncsu.edu/plants/pteridium-aquilinum/

Pteridium aquilinum (bracken fern):   Go Botany. (n.d.). https://gobotany.nativeplanttrust.org/species/pteridium/aquilinum/

Pteridium aquilinum (Bracken): Minnesota Wildflowers. (n.d.). https://www.minnesotawildflowers.info/fern/bracken

Quercus marilandica | Landscape Plants | Oregon State University. (n.d.). https://landscapeplants.oregonstate.edu/plants/quercus-marilandica

Quercus marilandica (Blackjack Oak, Oaks) | North Carolina Extension Gardener Plant Toolbox. (n.d.). https://plants.ces.ncsu.edu/plants/quercus-marilandica/

Quercus marilandica Blackjack Oak PFAF Plant Database. (n.d.). https://pfaf.org/user/Plant. aspx?LatinName=Quercus+marilandica

Ricinus communis - Plant Finder. (n.d.). https://www.missouribotanicalgarden.org/Plant Finder/PlantFinderDetails.aspx?taxonid=280095

Ricinus communis (African Wonder Tree, Castor Bean, Castor Bean Plant, Castor Oil Plant, Castor-oil Plant, Mole Bean Plant) | North Carolina Extension Gardener Plant Toolbox. (n.d.). https://plants.ces.ncsu.edu/plants/ricinus-communis/

Russula brevipes: The Ultimate Mushroom Guide. (n.d.). Mushroom Identification - Ultimate Mushroom Library. https://ultimate-mushroom.com/edible/868-russula-brevipes.html

Salit, R. B., Shea, Y. R., Gea-Banacloche, J., Fahle, G. A., Abu-Asab, M., Sugui, J. A., Carpenter, A. E., Quezado, M., Bishop, M. R., & Kwon-Chung, K. J. (2010). Death by Edible Mushroom: First Report of Volvariella volvacea as an Etiologic Agent of Invasive Disease in a Patient following Double Umbilical Cord Blood Transplantation. Journal of Clinical Microbiology, 48(11), 4329–4332. https://doi.org/10.1128/jcm.01222-10

Salvia rosmarinus - Plant Finder. (n.d.). https://www.missouribotanicalgarden.org/Plant Finder/PlantFinderDetails.aspx?kempercode=b968

Salvia rosmarinus (Anthos, Rosemary) | North Carolina Extension Gardener Plant Toolbox. (n.d.). https://plants.ces.ncsu.edu/plants/salvia-rosmarinus/

Sapindus drummondii | Landscape Plants | Oregon State University. (n.d.). https://landscape plants.oregonstate.edu/plants/sapindus-drummondii

Sapindus saponaria - Plant Finder. (n.d.). https://www.missouribotanicalgarden.org/Plant Finder/PlantFinderDetails.aspx?taxonid=286817&isprofile=0&

Sapindus saponaria Soapberry, Wild Chinaberry, Florida Soap Berry, Soap Nut, Soap Tree PFAF Plant Database. (n.d.). https://pfaf.org/user/Plant.aspx?LatinName=Sapindus+saponaria

Settevendemie, K. (2018, July 19). Indian Ricegrass (Achnatherum hymenoides) - Blackfoot Native Plants. Blackfoot Native Plants. http://blackfootnativeplants.com/BlackfootNative Plants/blackfoot-native-plants/indian-ricegrass-achnatherum-hymenoides/

Snow Fungus (Tremella fuciformis) | themyceliumemporium. (n.d.). Themyceliumemporium. https://www.themyceliumemporium.com/product-page/snow-fungus-tremella-fuciformis

Sophora secundiflora (Frijolillo, Mescal Bean, Mountain Laurel, Texas Mountain Laurel) | North Carolina Extension Gardener Plant Toolbox. (n.d.). https://plants.ces.ncsu.edu/plants/ sophora-secundiflora/

Sophora secundiflora Mescal Bean, Texas Mountain Laurel PFAF Plant Database. (n.d.). https:// pfaf.org/user/Plant.aspx?LatinName=Sophora+secundiflora

Species Spotlight: Celtis laevigata, Sugarberry | AustinTexas.gov. (n.d.). https://www.austin texas.gov/blog/species-spotlight-celtis-laevigata-sugarberry

Stevens, M. W. &. F. (n.d.-a). California Fungi: Calvatia booniana. https://www.mykoweb.com/ CAF/species/Calvatia_booniana.html

Stevens, M. W. &. F. (n.d.-b). California Fungi: Ganoderma applanatum. https://www. mykoweb.com/CAF/species/Ganoderma_applanatum.html

Stevens, M. W. &. F. (n.d.-c). California Fungi: Russula brevipes. https://www.mykoweb.com/ CAF/species/Russula_brevipes.html

Stevens, M. W. &. F. (n.d.-d). California Fungi: Tricholoma equestre. https://www.mykoweb. com/CAF/species/Tricholoma_equestre.html

Stropharia rugosoannulata. (2021, October 25). Midwest American Mycological Information. https://midwestmycology.org/stropharia-rugoso-annulata/

Stropharia rugosoannulata, Wine Roundhead mushroom. (n.d.). https://www.first-nature.com/ fungi/stropharia-rugosoannulata.php

Stubby brittlegill (Russula brevipes) - JungleDragon. (n.d.). JungleDragon. https://www.jungle dragon.com/specie/6984/stubby_brittlegill.html

Sturla, E. (n.d.-a). Lippia graveolens, Mexican Oregano, Southwest Desert Flora. http://south westdesertflora.com/WebsiteFolders/All_Species/Verbenaceae/Lippia%20grave olens,%20Mexican%20Oregano.html

Sturla, E. (n.d.-b). Monarda citriodora, Lemon Beebalm, Southwest Desert Flora. http://south westdesertflora.com/WebsiteFolders/All_Species/Lamiaceae/Monarda%20citri odora,%20Lemon%20Beebalm.html

Sturla, E. (n.d.-c). Vachellia farnesiana, (=Acacia farnesiana), Sweet Acacia, Southwest Desert Flora. https://southwestdesertflora.com/WebsiteFolders/All_Species/Fabaceae/Vachellia%20farnesiana,%20Sweet%20Acacia.html

Susan.Mahr. (n.d.). Castor Bean, <em>Ricinus communis. Wisconsin Horticulture. <span>https://hort.extension.wisc.edu/articles/castor-bean-ricinus-communis/

Texas Native Plants Database. (n.d.-a). https://aggie-hort.tamu.edu/ornamentals/nativeshrubs/mahoniatrifol.htm

Texas Native Plants Database. (n.d.-b). https://aggie-hort.tamu.edu/ornamentals/natives/RHUSLANCEOLATA.HTM

Texas Native Plants Database. (n.d.-c). https://aggie-hort.tamu.edu/ornamentals/natives/CRATAEGUSOPACA.HTM

Texas Persimmon(Diospyros texana). (2021, June 25). Alamo Area Chapter. https://txmn.org/alamo/area-resources/natural-areas-and-linear-creekways-guide/texas-persimmon/

The Editors of Encyclopaedia Britannica. (2023, March 2). Castor-oil plant | Description, Uses, & Ricin. Encyclopedia Britannica. https://www.britannica.com/plant/castor-oil-plant

Turker, A. U., & Gürel, E. (2005). Common mullein (Verbascum thapsus L.): recent advances in research. Phytotherapy Research, 19(9), 733–739. https://doi.org/10.1002/ptr.1653

Typha latifolia Reedmace, Broadleaf cattail, Bullrush, Nailrod PFAF Plant Database. (n.d.). https://pfaf.org/User/plant.aspx?LatinName=Typha+latifolia

USDA Plants Database. (n.d.). https://plants.usda.gov/home

Vaccinium arboreum (Farkleberry, Huckleberry, Sparkleberry, Tree Sparkleberry, Winter Huckleberry) | North Carolina Extension Gardener Plant Toolbox. (n.d.). https://plants.ces.ncsu.edu/plants/vaccinium-arboreum/

Vaccinium arboreum Farkleberry PFAF Plant Database. (n.d.). https://pfaf.org/user/Plant.aspx?LatinName=Vaccinium+arboreum

Veenstra, J. P. (2021). Rosemary (Salvia rosmarinus): Health-promoting benefits and food preservative properties. PubMed Central (PMC). https://www.ncbi.nlm.nih.gov/pmc/articles/PMC8513767/

Verbascum thapsus - Plant Finder. (n.d.). https://www.missouribotanicalgarden.org/PlantFinder/PlantFinderDetails.aspx?taxonid=287011

Verbascum thapsus Great Mullein, Common mullein, Aaron's Rod, Flannel Plant, Hag Taper, Mullein, Torches, Velvet Plant PFAF Plant Database. (n.d.). https://pfaf.org/user/plant.aspx?LatinName=Verbascum+thapsus

Verbena hastata American Blue Vervain, Swamp verbena PFAF Plant Database. (n.d.). https://pfaf.org/user/Plant.aspx?LatinName=Verbena+hastata

Virginia Tech Dendrology Fact Sheet. (n.d.). https://dendro.cnre.vt.edu/dendrology/syllabus/factsheet.cfm?ID=56

Vitis mustangensis. (n.d.). http://www.sbs.utexas.edu/bio406d/images/pics/vit/vitis_mustangensis.htm

Vitis mustangensis Mustang Grape PFAF Plant Database. (n.d.). https://pfaf.org/user/Plant.aspx?LatinName=Vitis+mustangensis

Vorderbruggen, M. M., PhD. (n.d.-a). Agarita. https://www.foragingtexas.com/2006/05/agarita.html

Vorderbruggen, M. M., PhD. (n.d.-b). Grape - Mustang. https://www.foragingtexas.com/2008/08/grape-mustang.html

Webmaster, A. (2023, February 24). Know Your Natives – Carolina Larkspur. Arkansas Native Plant Society. https://anps.org/2019/02/22/know-your-natives-carolina-larkspur/

western wheatgrass: Pascopyrum smithii (Cyperales: Poaceae): Invasive Plant Atlas of the

United States. (n.d.). https://www.invasiveplantatlas.org/subject.html?sub=22083

Wild Larkspur (Delphinium carolinianum) | ozarkedgewildflowers.com. (n.d.). https://ozarkedgewildflowers.com/plant-details/wild-larkspur-delphinium-carolinianum/

Yucca treculeana | Landscape Plants | Oregon State University. (n.d.). https://landscapeplants.oregonstate.edu/plants/yucca-treculeana

Yucca treculeana | The Cactus King. (n.d.). https://thecactusking.com/plants/all-plants/yucca-treculeana